To the Owen Family
May Gods grace
be upon you always
1/15/19

"THE OTHER FACE OF VICTORY"

"A dramatic testimony of faith built through suffering"

by Carlos and Miriam Peñaloza

The Other Face of Victory

Pastor Carlos Peñaloza

Illustration & Cover Design:

Mauricio Cespedes

Layout Design:

Salomon Paredes

All Bible verses taken from The Holy Bible

English Standard Version®

Category: Testimony

ISBN: 978-0-615-44788-9

Printed in Berryville Graphics

United States of America

Year: 2013

A production of: Ekklesia USA

Virginia, United States

www.ekkle.com / www.theotherfaceofvictory.com

e-mail: contacto@ekkle.com / info@theotherfaceofvictory.com

Telephone: 703-464-5877

DEDICATIONS

I want to dedicate this work to my wife, Miriam. Without her, this testimony would have not been possible.

She is my hero. I do not know anybody else like her that prays until she gets divine answers when she presents her burdens before the Lord. Her dedication, her focus, her sacrifice, and the attention to detail in everything she does. Dressed by the joy of the Holy Spirit, she puts her hands to work and makes everything with excellence. In regards to our children, she was the architect of their faith and their desire for eternity with Christ. Certainly she has achieved in the lives of our children everything that God had prepared for them.

I never heard a word of reproach during our difficult journey. She never questioned my leadership and when she went through all the suffering, she went through it silently taking refuge in the only one that can give us all the answers. Our Lord Jesus Christ.

Thank you my love for being the way you are and for persevering with me in our pilgrimage.

SPECIAL THANKS

In first place, I want to thank God, without his help this testimony would not have been possible.

My thanks to the staff of Ekklesia USA, that has been with us in all the process and preparation of the book. Special thanks to Silvia Daza for preparing the manuscript and to Salomon Paredes for his work in the preparation of this book.

Finally, my eternal gratitude to all the people that in the years of our lives have played a role in working of our testimony. To Miriam and I they are our angels of flesh and blood.

God bless you!

Pastor Carlos Peñaloza

Ekklesia USA, Reston VA

ENDORSEMENT

The book that you hold in your hands is one of those most challenging books that you could read.

I had the privilege to walk with Carlos and Miriam in the late 70's. Their faith has always inspired me just like it will inspire yours.

Very few have gone through circumstances like the ones they went through and very few have come out as pure gold as they have.

Thank you, Carlos and Miriam, for sharing your lives and testimony through this book.

Dick Iverson

Founder of Bible Temple (Currently City Bible Church)

Founder of Ministers Fellowship International

There are some people you meet and marvel at their unwavering faith in the midst of unimaginable crises. Carlos and Miriam are those people. Their gripping testimony of the sufficiency of God's grace on the mountains and in the valleys will surely inspire you to trust that in the midst of pain, God is the Good Shepherd and His strength is made perfect when we are not able to comfort ourselves or answer the thousands of questions swirling in our minds. Read this book and be challenged to unlock another level of understanding the inexhaustible grace of God that turns life's gritty situations into a message of peace and victory in Christ.

Frank Damazio

Lead Pastor, City Bible Church

Chairman, Ministers Fellowship International

COMMENTS

Some pain is simply indescribable. For those of us who haven't lost a child it's impossible to relate to that kind of experience. Here's the story of a couple who lost not one but all four of their children and they are able to say that God healed their pain and gave them the strength they needed to go on with their lives.

What an absolutely amazing story! I cannot even imagine going through that kind of pain. And what a testimony to the faithfulness of God!

The Bible teaches us that God is the God of all comfort and when you hear a story like that you know they had to receive supernatural comfort because it just seems like there's no way apart from God's help that they could now be having the great life they have and that they've had one hundred percent healing!

Joyce Meyer

TABLE OF CONTENTS

PROLOGUE

This is really an exceptional book particularly in light of the times in which we live.

I confess something to the reader. After having written the prologues of many books authored by friends both near and far, in this case I feel absolutely inept. It is a great honor for Carlos to extend an invitation to me to write a few words of introduction to this masterly work. Reading "The Other Face of Victory" was like hearing a majestic symphony.

The stories shared by Pastors Carlos and Miriam Penaloza read like a modern day version of the Book of Job.

How honest are their explanations! Carlos bares his heart, the heart of a true servant of God.

They transport us to peaks of glory whilst taking us through extraordinary memories: the awesome ministry of Julio Cesar Ruibal that not only shook Bolivia, but also burst through its borders; the tender relationships with their four precious children; the battles, the questions in the midst of trials that reached overwhelming extremes; the "angels" that ministered to their needs; the powerful miracles that they experienced; the sweet encounter between Daniela and Barney…and so many other things!

The photos of Carlos and Miriam toward the end of the book blessed me greatly. Are these not the faces of those who have passed through the fiery furnace? How beautiful they both look! There is so much peace on their faces.

While reading this book I felt like I was looking into the face of a giant.

Here is why I feel that this book is perfect for the times in which we live.
I fear that at this stage of Christian history, a disproportionate number of Christian personalities have arisen in the movie star style of Hollywood.

Much has been said of success, accomplishments and prosperity. Great emphasis has been placed on how much can be obtained. Perhaps that is why our Christianity does not transform society. It is superficial and has filled our congregations with people only seeking the "loaves and the fishes"; a bunch of spiritual children who catch pneumonia with the first breezes of the fall season.

This book clearly presents a forgotten facet of theology: suffering.

No matter how much we want to ignore it, suffering is a part of life. This book teaches us that character development is fundamental to Christianity.

We don't love God for what He gives us. We love Him and serve Him for who He is: the owner of all things, the supreme authority, the Sovereign One. He is everything to us.

Thank you, my beloved Pastors Penaloza, for being so sincere and open in sharing this glorious testimony. This book will dry the tears of many who are "in the valley of the shadow of death". Many will discover that even in the midst of pain, "He is the Good Shepherd", "Thy rod and thy staff, they comfort me".

I extend a warm welcome to "The Other Face of Victory; a book that everyone should read. This literary work will impart the strength of the Lord to your lives.

With great admiration,

Alberto H. Mottesi

"And he died for all, that those who live might no longer live for themselves but for him who for their sake died and was raised."

2nd Corinthians 5:15

INTRODUCTION

Ever since I began to serve the Lord, I have always had ministerial expectations and desires that included the smallest details and the grandest plans. As I matured in my walk with Christ and read the testimonies of others who served God and who were powerful instruments in His hands, my desires changed into one fervent desire to be a useful instrument for God for the cause of the gospel.

I was discipled through a young minister that was greatly used by God in the first and only revival experienced in Bolivia, with real signs and wonders, just like the Bible tells us had occurred in the early church. I understood that all things are possible in the name of Jesus because I had seen it with my own eyes. I had a real live example in the person of my pastor, Julio Ruibal, that it was possible to serve God and see biblical signs in the ministry and consequently, at that time it was perfectly natural for me to think and expect that my life would give glory to God under a prosperous, multitudinous and international ministry. As it turned out, all those things became a reality. I was part of one of the most fruitful ministries that God has lifted up in my generation in South America

Nonetheless, I completely ignored the fact that the plans of God are different than my plans. Without my knowing it, He had established that our testimony would serve as an inspiration, motivation and consolation for thousands of people, but not just through signs, wonders and a glorious ministry, but also through a life that would experience victory in the midst of extreme suffering. Through it I would receive consolation from the Holy Spirit of God that has no reasonable explanation and that surpasses all understanding. This is how Miriam and I came to understand that there are two faces to victory: One is the one we all know and want, success, miracles, signs and clouds of glory. The other is possibly the one that many of us know and accept but in no way desire...victory filled with loss and suffering, that does not produce applause, but rather a silence of admiration and adoration to Him who keeps the promise in His word,

"And we know that all things work together for good to them that love God, to them who are called according to his purpose."

Romans 8:28

One of the biblical texts that most impacted my life since I began to walk with the Lord is Hebrews chapter 11. There I learned in detail the names and the experiences of men and women who walked with God and who, due to their incomparable faith, wrote poetry and felt the power of the Most High operating in their lives and bestowing blessing upon their lives, their families and their communities. In that biblical text I not only understood the significance of true faith, but also the complex dimensions of the hand of God in any circumstance.

The first verses of the chapter take us through a path full of adventures and emotional events related to Abel, Enoch, Noah, Abraham, Sara, Isaac, Jacob, Joseph, Moses, Rahab the harlot and many others whose actions always resulted in developing a new dimension of faith. When I first read the details of these people, I closed my eyes and I began to deeply desire what they had. I would ask how would Moses have felt standing before the Red Sea with an army of Egyptians about to overtake them and God saying "Lift up thy rod!" and then to watch the sea open up and for him to walk leading three million people through it as on dry land. I would also ask myself how would it have been for Enoch to walk by God's side and talk with Him. I would ask so much more about those men who journeyed through violent fires and closed the mouths of lions. That is the face of victory that we all know and the one I wanted to experience. But upon reading verse 35 and beyond, in the same chapter 11 of Hebrews, I found something totally different: Many of these men and women were tormented, disgraced, tested and died by the sword and did not receive what was promised. Nonetheless, the Bible considers them Heroes of the Faith.

That, my dear readers, is **The Other Face of Victory**

I pray with all my heart that this testimony will motivate you to serve God without regard to circumstances, because He can turn the most terrible experience into the most brilliant victory. In the end, this painful side of victory, the same one experienced by our teacher and Lord, has been passed on for generations to all of us who are sealed with His Spirit and work under His authority.

Pastor Carlos Peñaloza

CHAPTER 1

THROUGH THE MIRACLE DOOR

"...So the last will be first, and the first last.""

Matthew 20: 16b

Before the thunderous applause of parents, friends and 20,000 other people, a few young 15-year-old athletes, participants in the La Paz Division of the National Soccer organization, circled the stadium carrying the championship trophy in Olympic style. They had trained and struggled for months to get to this moment on that day in Hernando Siles Stadium in La Paz, Bolivia.

It was truly the most exciting day of their lives especially for one young man, Carlos Penaloza.

Carlos had accomplished the first step toward achieving his coveted dream of becoming a professional player: to see the stadiums filled with people who shared the same passion, applauding like they themselves were the players...that was precisely his deepest desire.

However, two roads had developed in his life: one, the desire of his heart and the other the prophetic desire sketched out by his father and inspired from the heavens.

He remembered the words of his parents, when they recounted the details of that day when they slowly made their way down the cobble stone streets of the city of La Paz, Bolivia headed for the clinic where they sought confirmation of their first pregnancy.

Otilia, his mother, motioned toward her womb and said, " I would like for my son to become a successful professional, a doctor for example or an attorney."

Luis, his father, smiled and responded, "No. I want him to be something related with God."

Since the country was predominently catholic and intolerant of other religious beliefs, his mother assumed, "Oh, a bishop?"

His father who had never heard a single word about the gospel, said in his customary calm way, "No. Something related with God."

THE REVOLUTION

In those days Bolivia was a South American country best known for its revolutions that installed and removed Presidents with amazing frequency. As children we looked at this, at times, in awe and sometimes as just a natural process. But in the year 1972, in which the supernatural presence of God was made evident, there began the largest and greatest revolution that we would experience in our lifetimes.

The multitudes would gather to hear the words of a

young 19-year-old named Julio Ruibal[1]. He had heard of a powerful and marvelous God and had decided to give Him his life one year earlier under the ministry of Kathryn Kulhman[2], who was being used as a powerful instrument in preaching the gospel, with signs and wonders like those described in the Book of Acts.

---

1. Julio Ruibal: Described in the press as "The Apostle of the Andes" established one of the largest churches in his native La Paz, Bolivia. Later he moved to Cali, Colombia where he founded Ekklesia Colombia. He authored, "Anointed for the Endtime Harvest". He was assassinated in Cali, Colombia in 1995.

2. Kathryn Kulhman called "The Faith Healer" was born in Concordia, Missouri in 1907. She began to preach at age 16 and traveled throughout the United States conducting evangelistic and healing crusades. She directed a television program and wrote, "I Believe in Miracles" and "It's Never Too Late". She died in 1976 from complications following heart surgery.

Without any organization to back him or any financial support, Julio Ruibal had believed a message that God had given him in a Kathryn Kulhman crusade: "*Return to your country, and you will see that I will do the same signs and wonders through you. You will see the stadiums filled and many miracles and healings will occur because of what I will do through you.*"

Julio Ruibal had moved to the United States to study medicine. His sudden return to La Paz was a surprise to his father Cesar Ruibal who could not understand his conversion or his new activities.

"PREACHER OF THE GOSPEL!!????"

The message of Christ brought division to the family, an incomprehensible situation, since in our country no decent family ever considered even the possibility that one of its members would become a preacher of the gospel. It was simply not a consideration. Two things came to mind whenever the gospel was mentioned. The first was regarding the American and European missionaries whom most considered good people, but out of their mind. Who in their right mind would abandon their comforts at home and go to a foreign people to speak of an invisible God?

The second idea was that the gospel was commonly believed only among the rural indigenous people who were known to be less educated and believed to be unable to reason and, therefore, susceptible to influence and indoctrination. The city people who were educated and trained in the official religion could certainly not see themselves involved in either group which held any of these views.

It was in this environment that Cesar Ruibal threw his son out of his house and caused young Julio to seek refuge in the home of a friend. From there Julio began preaching the message of Jesus. A distinctive phrase would mark the new movement:

"JESUS LOVES YOU!"

A powerful movement of God would be necessary to break the centuries of bondage created by organized religion in our country. However, God's way of reaching His objectives and purposes are unimaginable to us.

Julio Ruibal formed a very large group of followers and he was accepted by some churches. He preached his messages with an extraordinary miracle power that was apparent to others. Then something happened that gave way to an explosion of the gospel in Bolivia.

An official in the government had been involved in a very serious accident in which he was paralyzed and expected to be in a wheel chair for the rest of his life. Among his inner circle of confidants was a man who had witnessed the miracles in one of Julio's crusades so he suggested that Julio be invited to pray for the injured man.

When Julio arrived, the hospital room of the government

official was crowded with doctors, nurses and friends of the injured man. The air was filled with curiosity, skepticism and perhaps even faith. Julio preached his simple message: "*Jesus loves you.*" Then he prayed for the paralyzed man.

An intense heat filled the place. The sick man began to shake. His bones creaked. Everyone was perspiring. Julio finished his prayer and left. Three days later, the man walked out of his hospital room completely healed.

This very powerful miracle became so well known in the highest circles of political power which caused the President of Bolivia, General Hugo Banzer Suarez, to be interested in meeting the young man who had performed this amazing wonder. A few days later, Julio found himself in the main office of the Governmental Palace before the President of the Republic of Bolivia testifying about the power of God and explaining the miracle of the government official. At the end of their meeting, President Banzer asked Julio how he could help him. Julio responded without fear or doubt saying:

"I ask three things, Mr. President. First: That you would authorize me to use all the soccer stadiums in the country to preach this message. Second: That the state-owned radio and television stations be allowed to transmit these messages and third: an airplane to take me from city to city."

The President, with a big smile on his face, instructed his secretary to draft a letter granting his requests.

Pastor Julio Ruibal in one of his crusades.

Julio was a young man who spent 7 or 8 hours a day in prayer and he was in such close communion with God that he was guided by Him in the smallest details of his daily life. After this famous miracle happened, he received instruction from the Lord to begin the crusades in the soccer stadium of the city of La Paz. There began a revival without precedent in Bolivia. Thousands of people were healed of the most terrible infirmities.

On the field of that stadium in that city countless orthopedic apparatuses were abandoned, as were crutches, wheel chairs, corrective shoes, etc. Hundreds of people would rise up on their own strength after being healed by the power of God. The press bore first-hand witness and documented many of the miracles. People would gather by the thousands, to the point that in the last crusade in the stadium, 25,000 people were counted, but outside there were 60,000 more trying to get in. This caused Julio to climb to the roof of the stadium to speak to the multitudes who had gathered. They were convinced of the reality that Jesus is alive, that He heals and He restores. Similar events occurred in other cities in the nation like Oruro, Cochabamba, and Santa Cruz. Then they transcended the Bolivian borders and spread to Peru, Brazil and Colombia.

"And these signs will accompany those who believe: in my name they will cast out demons; they will speak in new tongues; they will pick up serpents with their hands; and if they drink any deadly poison, it will not hurt them; they will lay their hands on the sick, and they will recover."

Mark 16:17-18

A DOORWAY OPENS

All of us come to the Lord using a door through which we pass to begin our journey with Him. Some begin through the doorway of repentance, others through the doorway of need, especially spiritual needs, etc. In my case, I began my walk with the Lord passing through the doorway of the miraculous.

When I was 17 years old I spent all my time practicing soccer which was my passion and my singular idol. I was beginning my university education in engineering, but I was completely convinced that I would soon be a professional soccer player…a star!

On July 20, 1973 after finishing a training camp, I felt a cold beginning to take hold of my body. I just wanted to get home and rest, but instead I went to my aunt and uncle's house who were preparing to attend a meeting with disciples of Julio Ruibal. They convinced me to go with them saying that I could be healed. Upon arriving at the meeting house on Rosendo Gutierrez street in the Sopocachi neighborhood, I saw a small group of youth and teens, singing and being moved by a power I could not understand.

I quickly caught sight of one person: Eduardo Espinoza. Immediately I wanted to flee the house...the memories flooded my mind. A couple of years before, during my years at Don Bosco School, I had seen that same young man threatening his younger brother. I couldn't hit him like I wanted to but from that day forward, we never missed an opportunity to provoke one another.

Finally, one day, we decided to settle our differences like men and we made our way to an area behind the school known as "El Rio". Each of us was accompanied by our respective team of followers. The walls of two houses formed an "L" where we and our band of followers arranged ourselves to form a perfect boxing ring. The match was set, two fights were scheduled. The grade school kids tangled with each other until one of them began to cry. The winner was triumphant.

It was our turn. We began sizing each other up and suddenly we heard a shout, "The Frog!" (Father Sabini's nick name). We all ran in every direction, looking for a place to hide. Father Sabini accompanied by two teachers had come looking for the offenders. I had hidden behind an old door that was leaning against a wall. Breathing rapidly with fear, I quickly found that behind me someone else had found the same hiding place. Our eyes met and there we were again, face to face, me and Eduardo. We quickly banded together to say that the fight was just a joke, but "The Frog" did not believe us.

The next day in front of the entire school, the principal announced that there had been a running of the "bulls" where some novices had tried out their fists. They sent us home to face our parents.

And here we were again, Eduardo and me, two years later, face to face, in that house where someone suddenly jumping from his wheelchair and jubilantly moving about, made me return to the reality of the moment. I definitely did not want to be there. Just seeing Eduardo made me feel uncomfortable, but something held me there. One of the youth approached me and asked, "Have you received the Holy Spirit?" I told him, "No". He offered, "Do you want to?" and upon accepting his invitation, he began to pray for me and I fell to my knees. Then I moved to another spot and another youth placed his hand on my forehead and prayed rebuking evil spirits. I coughed and began to pray in tongues. The first miracle of my life had occurred, but something else happened that I could not understand. The Lord had entered into my life to transform it and He did this in a very unusual way.

We were known as the "Deacons of Ruibal". We were youths between the ages of 15 and 21. We lived the miracles shown in the Bible and we believed the message of the New Testament literally. There was no reason to question it. What was written was evident in our present day and in our generation. We were not hampered by rules or leaders who might limit our believing with all our hearts what was written in the Word. Still, the most impressive thing was that our faith was not theory. It was real.

We lived daily experiencing the power of God as much in our own lives as in the lives of the people who joined us in the congregation. Our God was a God of miracles capable of the most amazing things like the case of one particular lady whose cancer had caused her doctors to give up on her. Her family had been summoned to her bedside where the very stench of her decomposing body was even bothersome to other patients around her. Her children had heard of the healing crusades being held at the soccer stadium and they purposed to take her there. She didn't understand even one word of what was happening since she only spoke her native Aymara, a language of the indigenous people of Bolivia.

That day Julio Ruibal preached, as always, with a supernatural anointing saying that God was healing someone of cancer. Immediately the woman got up, gathered her things and began to walk without assistance. The pain and her illness had disappeared! Although I was very young at the time, I had the privilege of knowing her and of witnessing her healing. She was later transformed into one of the most faithful assistants in the church.

"... there is in my heart as it were a burning fire shut up in my bones..."

Jeremiah 20:9b

Soccer had moved to second place in my life. I decided to abandon it and devote myself completely to serving Jesus Christ with His servant, Julio Ruibal. At times, our youth and inexperience worked against us and we made mistakes that affected the Lord's revival and the intensity of His visitations and the manifestation of His power diminished. However, the nation had already been shaken by God.

In February of 1974, the last large revival was held. Only 5,000 people gathered that day. Although the number of miracles was diminished, the same power of God was felt as from the beginning. It was in this environment that "Ekklesia Mision Boliviana", (Bolivian Mission Ekklesia) was born.

Preaching in the plazas of La Paz, Bolivia. 1976

Interestingly, more than 90% of the young followers were no longer with us. I was 17 years old at that time and I was one of the younger ones and one of the least experienced, but I became the closest collaborator to Julio and in 1977 along with three other brothers from the church, we traveled to the United States for theological training. This was made possible by scholarships granted through the leadership of Pastor Dick Iverson, whom more than anyone, was to become the greatest spiritual influence of my life.

Pastor Dick Iverson (left) and Carlos as a student at Portland Bible College (PBC).

After finally arriving at Portland Bible College, in Portland, Oregon in the United States, I was disquieted by a haunting detail. I called my pastor and said, "The classes are all going to be in Spanish, right?" "Are you crazy?" he said, "This is the United States! Here everything is in English!" said Julio Ruibal calmly. "So how am I going to do this if I only speak Spanish?" I asked. "You will have to ask God to help you" he replied.

Obediently, I prayed to God clinging to the words in *Mark 11:24* ,

"Therefore I tell you, whatever you ask in prayer, believe that you have received it, and it will be yours."

"Lord", I prayed, "I need your help. You have brought me here, but I can do nothing without a command of the English language. Please, do something!"

That week a family camp meeting had begun in the church. The prophet, Ernest Gentile preached in English. He spoke phrases that meant nothing to me. Again, I prayed to God:

"Lord, do something!"

The next day during the second conference, something happened inside of me. I began to understand some of the words. By the third day I understood a fourth of the message, the fourth day half of the message. On the fifth day I not only understood the message, but I memorized the entire message: "The ABC's of Marriage". God had done the miracle. I understood English in five days.

Once I began my classes I concentrated on understanding the instructors. Within a month I began taking notes in english and eventually I became bilingual.

Carlos Peñaloza at 18 years old

¿PASTOR?... ¡PASTOR!

"And he gave some, apostles; and some, prophets; and some, evangelists; and some, pastors and teachers; For the perfecting of the saints, for the work of the ministry, for the edifying of the body of Christ"

Ephesians 4: 11, 12

While I was studying I attended a prophetic event at Bible Temple in Portland and when those involved in prophetic ministry arrived, I expected that God would speak to me defining His desires for my life. Suddenly I felt a word that crossed my mind and planted itself in my heart: "Pastor!"

It was not what I wanted to do because I thought that pastors didn't do anything, but when I returned to Bolivia, I was

In 1995 Julio Ruibal was assassinated in Cali, Republic of Colombia and survived by his wife and two precious daughters who were, in my opinion, the fruit of a wonderfully complete and blessed marriage. I had the honor of presiding at his burial in farewell to his body and to return it to the earth knowing that his spirit is in the presence of God.

CHAPTER 2

FROM A GOOD GIRL TO A GIRL OF GOOD

"Or do you not know that your body is a temple of the Holy Spirit within you, whom you have from God? You are not your own, for you were bought with a price. So glorify God in your body."

1 Corinthians 6:19, 20

I know that when God chooses you to serve Him, He also chooses the one who will share your life with you. That's the way it was with Miriam, my wife, who a couple of years after I was saved, had also experienced a profound transformation in her life.

She was in every sense of the Bolivian expression, "a nice girl". An only daughter, and the center of attention for her parents, she enjoyed all the benefits of living under their roof. At 20 years old she was studying at the local university and she was reaching one of her goals: to have a career and to work towards getting to the highest possible level of her profession. She loved parties and had many suitors, but she could not find purpose in her life, and she felt that her heart was empty, darkened by loneliness and depression that once in a while led her to wish she was dead.

She tried to have spiritual experiences by praying to religious statues that she was told would give her internal peace, or she would attend conferences with a transcendental meditation guru. However, everyday she became more and more convinced that her life had no meaning.

Miriam had a university friend named Marcelo, who had been unjustly accused in a legal matter and sent to prison. As soon as he was given the miracle of freedom, he felt in his heart that he could not let another day go by without also ushering his friend, Miriam, towards the spiritual liberty that she needed. Although when he was released, he was broken and somewhat lost, he immediately went to Miriam's house along with Jorge Villavicencio, a Christian brother who was to provide great assistance to us later.

Jorge spoke to Miriam about the Lord and she received Him in her heart while experiencing an incomparable peace in her life. Until that night, Miriam had suffered from insomnia and would spend the night chain-smoking cigarettes. After that day, every time she wanted to light up a cigarette, she would begin to cough. She never again had insomnia or felt the need to return to smoking.

For three months, Marcelo and Jorge taught Miriam the Word of God, but despite these experiences and since human beings are creatures of habit, she continued in her old ways maintaining her old lifestyle, believing that dedicating sporadic moments to God was sufficient. Jorge lost his patience; Marcelo confronted her pushing her toward a decision: carry on as you were before or serve the Lord. The word of God became imbedded in the deepest recesses of Miriam's heart.

In a public park, before a stone bench, Miriam knelt, poured out her heart before the Lord and genuinely gave her life to Him.

"Be sober-minded; be watchful. Your adversary the devil prowls

around like a roaring lion, seeking someone to devour."

1 Peter 5:8

The entire way home, Miriam cried because she felt a profound conviction that she had sinned. Nonetheless, when she tried to sleep, the devil would appear to her in person in her room saying, "I will not leave you alone because you belong to me!" She was greatly troubled. The enemy was extremely close, threatening and inclined to do anything to accomplish his purposes. There she learned to use her faith, and crying she cried out to the Lord, "Lord, help me. Do not let the devil take me! I want to belong to you, Lord!"

She wrestled and cried out for hours and with each passing moment she became more convinced that she had made the right decision by giving her life to Jesus. She wouldn't go back on it!

At five in the morning victory came. The adversary could no longer torment her now that this, "nice girl" had decided to follow Christ. From that moment forward, Miriam felt different. She began to faithfully attend services at the church and to take the first steps of her Christian life. To this day she yields and is consecrated to God, rising above great trials as a woman, wife, mother and minister of God.

In 1976 Miriam held an important responsibility as an Executive Secretary of a governmental agency in our country. One day, Pastor Ruibal asked for her cooperation as secretary of an evangelistic campaign that was about to happen. She didn't have to think about it.

She asked for three months leave of absence to handle

the administrative and organizational responsibilities of the crusades. Her love for the service of the Lord would lead her to do more than she had expected to when Pastor Ruibal invited her to take a permanent position in the church - an invitation which Miriam considered a great honor.

"Blessed is the one you choose and bring near, to dwell in your courts! We shall be satisfied with the goodness of your house, the holiness of your temple!"

Psalms 65:4

When Miriam notified her employer that she was leaving her position, he knew that she was receiving a good salary and that her pastor had made it clear that what she would receive at the church would be much less. He thought she had lost her mind saying, "For God's sake!! What has Pastor Ruibal done to you?! Consider your future! You are very young and you have a successful future ahead of you!" But she could only think of the God she loved and whom she would serve the rest of her life.

Miriam as secretary of Ekklesía Bolivia, 1977

Once at the church, she not only worked in administrative matters, but in spiritual matters as well. She was part of the choir, served as worship leader, and visited the imprisoned and the sick in hospitals. She served as the Sunday School teacher for the children, counselor to young people and grew into a role as an evangelical worker. The pastor placed her in all available areas of work as became necessary. However, her ministerial calling was not yet defined.

Years later, the Lord showed her that everything she had learned to do had been part of her preparation to become a pastor herself.

CHAPTER 3

TAKE WIVES AND HAVE SONS AND DAUGHTERS

[6]But seek the welfare of the city where I have sent you into exile, and pray to the Lord on its behalf, for in its welfare you will find your welfare"

Jeremiah 29: 6a, 7

From 1973 I began serving full time in the ministry and four years later, Miriam joined us working in our church offices.

Years later once I was ordained as a Pastor, the work and preparation of church activities provoked a closeness between us leading my heart to have special feelings towards her.

Months later Miriam went to work with Pastor Ruibal to Colombia and we did not see or write to one another for a year. Then I had an opportunity to go to Colombia and see her again only to discover that our hearts had not changed one bit during our separation. I formally asked her to marry me. I asked, "Do you want to marry me?" With such an unexpected question I caused Miriam to fast and pray for one week before she gave me her answer. She spoke to God this way,

"Lord, if it be your will that I marry Carlos, I want you to clearly confirm it. I want you to specifically say to me, 'Get married'". She wanted to do the will of God. She had made the decision to move completely in His will.

On the designated day, Miriam again said to the Father, *"I need a specific word from you Lord."* and upon opening her

Bible, the Lord took her to verse 6 of chapter 29 in Jeremiah:

"Take wives and have sons and daughters..."

The marriage was confirmed! However, in that same chapter, God showed her that we would be returning to our country at the same time:

"and will bring you back to the place from which I carried you into exile..."

Jeremiah 29:14b

We were engaged in February of 1983 and we made the preparations and the plans for a two month period. On May 7 of the same year we arrived at the altar.

Our resources were very limited, but the love of the brethren allowed us to enjoy a beautiful albeit simple ceremony in the presence of almost all the congregation in Cali Colombia. The final ceremonial words of Pastor Ruibal, *"...for better or worse, in sickness and in health, until death do you part"* sealed our destiny.

After the ceremony, a joyous caravan paraded the streets of the city along with the beaming couple. We were overjoyed. We had never imagined that we would be starting a new life so far away from home. We also never imagined that this was the beginning of a difficult journey that would take us step by step through the other face of victory.

Carlos and Miriam on their wedding day.

Cali Colombia. 1983

CHAPTER 4

WOE TO HIM WHO STRIVES WITH HIM WHO FORMED HIM

"a pot among earthen pots! Does the clay say to him who forms it, 'What are you making?'or 'Your work has no handles'?"

Isaiah 45:9

After some years of living in Colombia, we came to love that country. Nonetheless, the situation in Ekklesia Colombia had become unsustainable. Everything that pertained to the congregation had to go through the consideration of the pastor and even personal matters had to receive his approval. The results were differences among us that became rigid and legalistic.

A GREAT RESPONSIBILITY ON IT'S WAY!

Three months after we married, we received the wonderful news that we were to become parents and since our income was barely enough to cover the rent where we lived, I had to find a job in order to sustain my family. God covered the rest of our needs with the help of several of the brethren who generously offered us whatever was at their disposal. Soon I obtained part time employment as an English teacher. I had to provide food for my wife and the little one that God was placing in our hands to care for, love and mold and even to prepare him to be inclined to serve the Lord. With this new job, working only 4 hours a day, we were making in 15 days what we woud have earned in one month at church.

Miriam left her job at the church at my suggestion. I felt that the Lord wanted to take her to a new dimension of faith and show her that I could cover all the needs of our home.

Due to our differences, Pastor Ruibal called us into a meeting during which we were asked to leave the church. He made it clear that there was no possibility of continuing our relationship with Ekklesia Colombia or Ekklesia Bolivia. We left in peace. A few days later we were asked to give back our furniture and other items that belonged to the church and finally the contract for our apartment was cancelled. We began a new congregation and worked hard to form the "Community of Love" which had grown quickly.

Later, Pastor Jorge Villavicencio took charge of the church, taking it to a new level. As of this writing it now has 14,000 members.

JOSE ESTEBAN IS BORN

The desire of Miriam's heart was to have many children and create a large and happy family.

I come from a family of 4 brothers and 1 sister. So when I was single I asked the Lord if one day He would grant me the blessing of being a father, that He should give me a daughter. For some reason the idea of having a daughter made me very happy.

The public health system in Cali, Colombia was such that the women who gave birth naturally were sent to a center where they offered only what help was necessary. In case of an emergency they were then transferred to a central hospital.

In the days leading up to the birth, Miriam was feeling fine. The 17th of May, 1984 was a beautiful day and we were confident that everything would be fine....but there were complications and she was sent by ambulance to the university hospital.

While I waited in the hallway, something happened that produced a special feeling in me: the sky suddenly became overcast and a storm broke out so fiercely that it caused me to ask the Lord, "What does this mean just as my wife is giving birth?" I did not receive any response and I continued waiting until a few minutes later the nurse came out to tell me that a son had been born with a beautiful jaw line. In my heart I felt a momentary disillusionment something like, "Oh well", because I was expecting a daughter.

Miriam came out on a gurney with the child lying on her lap, she looked tired, but happy. She was the proud mother of a son that was the desire of her heart. I looked at the child and was surprised at his prominent nose and his jaw line neither of which pleased me. Later as I looked at myself in the mirror, I understood from whom my beautiful son had inherited those prominent features.

We arrived at home very happy, but a breakdown in the health of our son forced us to hospitalize him. He had jaundice and required light therapy. This was the first of countless medical appointments and hospitalizations which became part of the process that God had chosen for us - to create a testimony in us in the midst of our suffering.

"...and I will bring you back to the place from which I sent you into exile.."

Jeremiah 29: 14b

As it is with many ministers, our lives were intrinsically linked with the church and while Jose Esteban grew, we continued the work and with it our expectations of a new life as a family. We counted on some of the brethren who worked with us, but like the Bible says ***"...their ways are not your ways"***. When we thought about the work in Colombia, the Holy Spirit spoke clearly to my heart telling me to return to Bolivia. He told me that my sheep awaited me there. I responded: *"I don't have any sheep there"* because in the agreement with Julio Cesar Ruibal, we had established that I was completely separated from the church in Bolivia.

Should we return to our country with it's narrow cobblestone streets where we did not enjoy a stable political or economic climate? Return to live in the cold mountain region, in the city built in the crater of a volcano, below the Illimani, that majestic snow covered mountain that kept watch over the city of La Paz? Impossible! The Holy Spirit's insistence was such that I began to pray like this, *" I understand that it is your will that I return to Bolivia, but I don't have any intentions of returning, I have nothing there, so if you want me to do this, you will have to kick me out of here"* .

Such a challenge to a merciful and loving God bore its fruit. Someone had turned me in to the immigration authorities. Having only a student visa, I was not eligible to have any kind of paid employment, but my stubbornness had been cemented by sentimental rationalizations and I had convinced myself that Miriam would agree with me. We wanted to stay in Colombia for lots of reasons. We had married there and our first child was born there.

I had passed the exam to work at another institute as

an instructor which allowed me to present all of the necessary documentation to continue living in Colombia. I arrived at the immigration office with all of the required documents, however, the Chief Immigration Officer responded, *"I will not give you one more day to stay in this country. If you stay, we will deport you and you will not be allowed to reenter the country!"* Not even the fact that my son was Colombian softened his heart. *"The baby can stay,"* he said, *"but you must go!"*

Miriam left Cali with the baby and traveled by air to the Colombian-Ecuadorian border. I travelled by ground all night carrying our 13 suitcases. I felt the hand of God on my back, kicking me out of Colombia and responding to my challenge.

When we met at the border, Miriam was to continue to La Paz, but the trip with the baby had been so difficult that she decided to continue the journey with me - come what may. And so it was that we began our journey back to Bolivia.

Our son enjoyed every minute of it, because he spent the whole time safely in the arms of his father and his mother. We were on the highway almost 12 hours a day so we could then rest in a hotel on the way. The money we had with us was sufficient. Miriam and I enjoyed being together as a family during the trip.

Our objective was to arrive in Bolivia, finish our university studies, live a life as professionals and serve as assistants in a church. However, God is God, and even though we are as humans, He handles our issues lovingly taking us toward restoration. We had learned some good lessons from our pastor. We had been trained to recognize the voice of God and to be sensitive to His guidance.

CHAPTER 5

IF YOU FAITHFULLY OBEY THE VOICE OF THE LORD YOUR GOD

"being careful to do all his commandments that I command you today, the Lord your God will set you high above all the nations of the earth. 2 And all these blessings shall come upon you and overtake you, if you obey the voice of the Lord your God."

Deuteronomy 28:1,2

Having mixed feelings about leaving Colombia and what awaited us in Bolivia, we travelled those 12 days on the highway passing the various cities of Ecuador and Peru and finally arriving in Bolivia. Our country was experiencing the worst economic crisis with a devaluation of 24000% annually. This caused a hyperinflation that produced dramatic changes politically and socially.

Approaching Bolivia, the voice of the Lord spoke to my heart one more time saying, *"When you arrive don't start a new church, get a job and dedicate yourself to your family"*. I felt humiliated by the way the Lord had taken me out of Colombia, so I simply obeyed.

"I, even I, have spoken and called him; I have brought him, and he will prosper in his way."

Isaiah 48:15

In reality He had already arranged things for us. Two days before we arrived, a friend called my mother to ask about me saying she had a job for me. I reached out to her as fast as I could and two days later I found myself working for World Vision-Bolivia. World Vision is a Christian humanitarian organization that works with children and families around the world.

EKKLESIA AGAIN

The Lord has His way and defines our path. He had called, chosen, and prepared us for His work. While I worked at World Vision, one day one of the leaders of Ekklesia showed up and invited me to a meeting. They wanted to know why we had returned to Bolivia. We prayed over the invitation to the meeting and Miriam and I were in agreement. We would do what the Lord wanted.

We arrived to a divided congregation diminished by dictatorial rules and greatly influenced by imposed legalism. There were barely 150 members and all of them were not happy with our presence there, so the Holy Spirit guided us to wait a year-and-a-half before returning to full time ministry. During this time the Lord walked us through a difficult period to establish the authority necessary to minister with Alberto and Silvia Salcedo. Later we would partner with them to form the Ekklesia team of pastors.

"The least one shall become a clan, and the smallest one a mighty nation; I am the Lord; in its time I will hasten it.. "

Isaiah 60:22

We entered into a new dimension of growth. We had healing and miracle services. Being now 300 members, the voice of the Lord said to me that we were going to be 5,000. We proclaimed it with full conviction. "How many are we?" we would ask and the multitude responded one more time, "Five thousand!".

Convinced that it was God who spoke to us, we decided to take a step of faith, to buy a theatre in which to meet. Until that time the banks had never lent money to a church and we had to go through many difficulties to get it. When we finally got the loan, it was the Lord himself who gave me the name for that auditorium, "La Casa de la Casa" ("The House of the House").

Ultimately, God gave us access to the media and we were able to obtain a radio station. Thousands of people had the opportunity to hear the messages and the worship services. In a short time the Lord opened doors for another massive communications channel through T.B.N. (Trinity Broadcasting Network) by which we were able to reach almost all the households in the country.

Without a doubt, God was fulfilling His promise. Every day we said to ourselves, *"It has been worth everything we have gone through."*

"... that he might humble you and test you, to do you good in the end...."

Deutoronomy 8:16b

Our son, little Jose, as we called him, was a happy child. Everyone in the family loved him and he became the favorite grandchild of his maternal grandfather. At six months of age he developed an allergy to his mother's milk so that he had to be fed soy milk.

When it was time for him to begin to walk, we noticed that he had trouble keeping his balance and controlling his saliva. We attributed this to teething, but after a year his doctors could not figure out what was the problem and they told us to just wait until he was older.

In 1986 Jose Esteban was almost 3 years old, when we were again blessed with another member of the family. The 20th of February we received a great gift from heaven, our daughter, Carla Gabriela. God had granted me the desire that I always had of becoming the father of a baby girl. Joy flooded our lives. Now we were complete, we were a stable marriage with a flourishing ministry and a couple of children who had stolen our hearts. What else could I ask God for?

What I didn't know was that with the arrival of Carla also came experiences that would affect our lives, our faith and our relationship with God; trials that we would not be able to withstand relying solely on our own strength. Without a doubt, it was the supernatural power of God that sustained us in every moment.

CHAPTER 6

CARLA: THE SACRIFICE OFFERING

The extraordinary things that God was doing with Ekklesia made the church full of the Holy Spirit. "The House of the House" was a place where everyone could be a witness to the supernatural through the power of God. It was evident that God was with us. However, at our door was one of the greatest tests that Miriam and I would have to live through both individually and as a couple.

"...and do not hinder them, for to such belongs the kingdom of heaven."

Matthew 19:14b

As soon as the doctor told us it was a girl, my heart soared with great joy and to see her, my soul was bound to her. As soon as she was born, I loved that child like nothing or nobody in the world. For some reason when I dreamed of having children, I had a tremendous desire to have a girl and Little Carla was my dream come true. I clung to her in such a way that after God, my life began to revolve around her - my comings and goings, my desires and aspirations. My efforts, in addition to being focused on the Lord's work, were otherwise solely directed toward caring for, caressing, loving and protecting my daughter. I completely gave myself over to making sure that she would be, from her earliest months, a healthy person, properly raised and sensitive to the voice of the Lord. Carla inhabited my heart so profoundly that I was ready to leave everything behind if her spiritual growth or well being required it. She was the answer to my prayer to become the father of a girl because as soon as she came into the world, she awoke in me the most pure and wondrous of emotions. Even though I already had a son whom I also loved, I felt complete as a father when Carla came into our lives. As soon as I took her into my arms, I cared for her, treating her with the utmost of tenderness. I changed her clothes and bathed her when necessary offering all the care that she required. From her earliest months I had already fashioned her future.

I planned to raise her to faithfully serve the Lord. I thought that as she grew up she would have the most beautiful voice like her mother and that she would sing for the Lord. One day, I thought someone would come along who would want to marry her, but the requirements would be something like this. He would have to be someone person completely consecrated and anointed by the one true God. Besides having planted a minimum of 20 churches, he would have had to been used in the resurrection of at least a dozen people. In a few words, *"Woe to him who dares to set his eyes on my daughter!"* She was only a few months old and I had her entire life already planned. When I thought of her my prayer to God was something like this: *"Lord, thank you for having given me the most beautiful little girl that any man could want as a daughter. I don't know what you have placed in her but she is the most precious little thing I have ever known. Help me to be a good provider so that she will lack for nothing. Forgive me for loving her more than anyone in my life. Help me not to idolize her or place her above You and give me more strength to raise her for You."* I was able to live through any difficult situation, but if my daughter was fine, nothing else mattered. They could throw me out of the church, but if I had my daughter with me, it wouldn't have mattered. She was the center of my attention, the motivation for my life and the cause of my praises to God. I had never felt such an intense love for any person and she was the most perfect gift that God could have ever given me.

There was nothing else that I wanted in life except to be close to my beloved daughter. I loved my wife and Jose, my firstborn, but I had to make a distinct effort not to unbalance the family and my relationship with them because Carla didn't have to do anything for me to love her: her pure existence consumed my attention. I give thanks to God for my wife for having been so patient with me, for having occupied herself with the one whom she loved greatly, our son, Jose. Miriam had to assume her role as mother and wife and correct and teach our little girl who proved to have a strong character very different from her older brother who, quite the contrary, was docile and tender-hearted.

Due to the birth of Carla, Miriam had to dedicate extra time to family commitments and reduce her ministerial activities. The two children demanded her presence each day more and more. This was specially true when difficulties began to emerge due to their genetic deficiencies which began to attack them relentlessly.

Carlita 6 months old

"Heal the sick, raise the dead, cleanse lepers, cast out demons: you recieve without paying; give without pay."

Matthew 10:8

Carla began to grow along with the church. The anointing of the Spirit never failed to manifest in the ministry and each time we were sure that we had entered into a "period of grace" that would usher in a new move of the Spirit that had not been experienced until that time in Bolivia. Thousands of people would be impacted by the presence of God just by entering into the building and their tears would be the immediate evidence that they felt it.

Ekklesia Bolivia "House of the House"

When we prayed for the sick, they were healed. Cancer left their bodies and people with incurable diseases of the brain, kidneys and the liver were restored immediately. It didn't matter what kind of ailment or how long they had been dealing with these infirmities, we simply asked God to intervene and the anointing for healing descended to accomplish the miracle.

Whatever God had given us we shared with everyone

who came needing an emotional, spiritual or physical miracle. The Holy Spirit would visit us in every service in an extraordinary manner. I reached a level of recognition and respect that is every pastor's dream.

THE PROPHECY

As happens with all growing ministries, God sends people anointed by Him that can strengthen and help establish it, and that also happened with us. One day two ministers visited us from Brazil. One of them had a rare gift. This woman would read one portion of the Scriptures revealed to her by the Lord and according to the text she would receive revelation regarding the lives of individuals. While we prayed with her, she said to me, "Brother, the Lord has given me a word for you. May I give it?" This was a challenge for me because by then I had encountered many false prophets who for attention's sake or to collect offerings or simply to occupy the pulpit, they would offer prophecies that simply lacked biblical substance or were not supported by the Lord. With all this in mind, I listened with reservation.

She said to me: *"Yes, brother, the Lord also told me that you would not accept me easily, but I want you to know that with much fear I will give you the message anyway."* She read the text from one of the Psalms and she started to tell me what God had for me. She began with general things that I had already heard many times, "*God loves you...you are a servant of the Lord...*" but then she continued with some details that began to capture my attention. "*God has revealed to me that you have suffered enough and much harm has been done to you and that you have asked God to seek vengeance, but that is not your business. God will judge in His time. Do not ask for this.*" Incredibly the Lord had shown her hidden feelings that I had not mentioned even to my wife. Then she began to speak of the future. *"I see a great trial coming into your life. There is a dark cloud over you. That cloud represents something that will greatly affect you. It will affect you in such a way that you will think that God has abandoned you. But you must know that it is not so, the Lord is telling you beforehand so that when this happens, you will know that He has shown it to you. He says that He shall take you by the hand and take you out of this trial. He is with you. The other thing I see is that you are giving an offering that is very, very big".* I thought that God would prosper me in such a financial way I would give a great deal of money to His work. But she clarified that it was not about money. *"You will give God an offering so great as your own life."*

The Lord used her also to tell me that I should warn the people telling them that they should pray before eating because an epidemic was on its way through the food chain. This epidemic would cause even death, but no one in the church would be affected if they obeyed this instruction. I believed what she said to the point that I informed the congregation and in fact two years later a cholera epidemic entered through Peru and affected other countries in South America including Bolivia, but the people in the church were completely unaffected by it.

Up until this time I could not imagine what the dark cloud over my life meant and I was even more confused about what was that very big offering that I was to give to God.

"To you, O Lord, I cry, and to the Lord I plead for mercy:"

Psalms 30:8

Jose Esteban was about 3 ½ and Carla 1 ½. It was 1988 and

the church was at the height of the visitation of the Spirit and we were a happy family and blessed in every way.

One day I arrived home and found that Carla was complaining of a pain in her stomach and she had a mild case of diarrhea as well. We took her to the doctor who thought the trouble was something common to children. He prescribed a medicine and the child quickly recovered.

A few days later we went on a trip with the youth of the church, a beautiful experience that lasted 10 days, but the stomach pain and the diarrhea returned. Again we went to her doctor who after examining her, ordered lab tests to find the cause of the problem. He was able to get her symptoms under control but he was unable to find any answers to her condition. One month later Carla got sick again, but this time the problem was more serious and we had to hospitalize her. Weeks passed and there was no solution.

My wife had to live with the usual questions that are typical with this kind of situation and face the difficulties and inconveniences of the hospital like the lack of care by some nurses and the insensitivity of some doctors. From Monday to Friday, Miriam stayed in that place, always with the hope of recovery. I would visit her several times a day. On Saturday I would replace her at the hospital and she would go home to attend to Little Jose who while under the care of his grandmother, suffered the absence of his mother and his little sister.

For nearly four months our movements were limited to a cycle of home-church-hospital. As a family we entered into a very grave crisis because we did not understand what was happening to our daughter. The church both inside and outside of Bolivia became aware of the situation and they began to pray for her asking God for a miracle.

Two months later they had to move Carla to intensive care. The doctors asked for medications that were unavailable in our country, but I looked for ways to get them anyway. Pastor Johnny Dueri brought various containers of intravenous feedings because our daughter could no longer eat by mouth. Like him, many other brothers would help me by bringing expensive medications many times without charging us for them. We intensified our seeking God in prayer and in various places all over the world people prayed for the daughter of the pastor who had a mega church in Bolivia. Benny Hinn prayed for her from afar. Yiye Avila prayed for her sending an anointed handkerchief, like so many other ministers, but our daughter would not get well. She was losing weight and became so weak as to become acutely malnourished. The left side of her body became paralyzed. Her body did not respond to the medications and the doctors offered no explanations.

My beloved mother, upon seeing our little daughter paralyzed on her left side said to me:

"Son, what are you going to do with her in this condition? The child is suffering greatly and your wife also. You are the one that is keeping her alive by your love for her. Why don't you let her go? It is too much suffering for you and for the entire family".

I told her I would fight for her until the last moment; I didn't care if she was paralyzed, even if I had to carry her in my arms for the rest of my life. I didn't just love her healthy body, I loved her! She was just too precious to me to let her go. If I could have given my life for her, I would have done it. My beloved mother could not handle so much suffering and stopped visiting her in the hospital because once the child motioned toward the door asking with gestures to be let out of that place. She could no longer continue seeing her granddaughter in agony and her son doing the impossible to keep her alive and her daughter-in-law daily battling such a hardship.

By this point we had received all kinds of opinions, suggestions, even accusations and comments regarding the health of our daughter. Some would even be so bold as to say that we were going through this trouble as the fruit of some curse or something similar, or that God was punishing us for the problems we had with our pastor in the past, but we just kept going forward.

CHAPTER 7

ANOTHER BATTLE: AS TOLD BY MIRIAM

Due to the unending bouts of diarrhea, Little Carla was assigned to a rehydration unit of the hospital, but first they sent us to a common area where other children were cared for who suffered the same problem. Like a good Christian mother I accompanied my little girl with the assurance that God would heal her and every day I cared for her with hope and with much love.

After a few days of being hospitalized, another little girl arrived with the same symptoms. Her name was Rosita. She was almost the same age as my daughter but she came from an orphanage. She had no parents or relatives who cared for her. This made me very sad and while my daughter slept I would get close to Rosita to speak to her, but one day one of the nurses sternly called me out. Since the illnesses of patients in that ward were highly contagious, I could not get close to anyone of them as they could compromise my health or make my daughter more ill. So I limited myself to watching Rosita from afar and praying for her.

I stayed by my daughter's crib 24 hours a day always watchful. I slept on a small sofa next to her crib but I could not see any improvement from the intravenous treatments that were constantly being administered, each time requiring a fresh puncture wound in different parts of her body.

Our daughter began to lose weight so as to remind me of the images of nude children in Africa. Her little bald head shined, all her little bones could be easily seen due to her emaciation and she had a bloated belly.

This particular Friday the doctors decided to introduce tubes into her nasal passages. They also took the opportunity of training me to care for her so that later on I could feed her through them, but as night approached our daughter went into shock. Her stomach became hard as a rock and she could not stop crying. The doctors on duty had left and only the medical residents were now available. When I called them they looked at my daughter and gave me contradictory opinions. Some said it was colic and others decided that it looked like her intestines were strangulated and that she needed surgery immediately.

They began to call the surgeon, the pediatrician, and the anesthesiologist and everyone who had to help with the surgery. All this while my little girl screamed with pain. I was very anguished and did not know what to do. Until this moment I had been emotionally strong and very careful in every detail of her care. My daughter did not have the slightest skin rash that all the other children experienced who had constant diarrhea because I took it upon myself to bathe her and hydrate her every day. However, neither my love nor my care could free her from the pain that she was suffering now and this was something for which I was not prepared. Finally, after two hours of crying and commotion, the doctors injected her with a strong sedative and they decided to wait. They told me that they couldn't guarantee that Carla would live. She stopped crying, but in that moment the greatest crisis of faith of my life began.

I began to cry and complain to the Lord asking why He was not healing my daughter..."What have I done to deserve this if from my youth I have served you and I have consecrated myself completely to you. I got married in your will, with a word from God, with confirmation in prayer and fasting, with confirmation of my pastors. What is this punishment that I am living if I trust in you?"

All I had was anguish and desperation in me. "How unjust are you with me! Even Rosita who is an orphan, a child that no one misses, who has no one to care for her...even she has gotten better and is ready to be released; and my daughter who is loved and cared for by her parents, you're not healing?!"

I cried for hours telling God so many things. Finally I exploded and I said to Him, "I don't believe in you anymore! I am completely angry with you for what you are doing! I don't want to have anything more to do with you!"

When I finished saying these things, I felt the Holy Spirit leave me and a heavy weight fell over me. Everything that up until now had been bearable was no longer. The anguish and the pain had enslaved me. I felt the same emptiness as when I did not know Him, that emptiness of spiritual death, the emptiness of being separated from God.

There was no hope left. Everything had ended and the only thing I could think of was dying. Dying and taking my daughter with me so she wouldn't suffer anymore. Only thoughts of suicide occupied my mind. I thought of ways to end my life and began to look for things that would help me accomplish that end. I understood that many used suicide as a solution to their problems. They have no hope. Neither do they have God and they see death as the only remedy. But what they don't see in reality is that when they die they begin a life separated from God for eternity. This is what the Bible calls the second death, the one from which Jesus Christ came to save us.

There were only a few mothers sleeping at the bedsides of their children and I tried to quietly enter into the place where they kept the medications so I could take something to end my life and that of my child's. I passed the entire night in this condition. I was exhausted. I did not know what to do.

Soon I looked out the window as the sky began to fill with light. I fell to my knees and crying out to the Lord I recognized my tremendous error.

"I cannot live without you and much less die without you. I love you...I need you. Forgive me!!... I repent with all my heart of all the words I spoke to you. Have mercy on me!!"

I was on the floor begging Him and crying. An hour must have passed until I began to clearly feel that He was forgiving me and cleansing me of all evil. His word was fulfilled:

"If we confess our sins, he is faithful and just to forgive us our sins, and to cleanse us from all unrighteousness."

1 John 1:9

Glory to God that His word is truth!!!!!!

Immediately I felt the Holy Spirit descend over me once more and I said to Him: *"I will serve you the rest of my life even if you don't heal my daughter. I love you more than life and more than anyone in this life and I accept your will whatever it may be because your will is always best."*

When we accept the will of God, however difficult it may seem, He always strengthens us supernaturally. I understood in a more profound and real way what it means to love God in all things.

"For I am sure that neither death nor life, nor angels nor rulers, nor things present nor things to come, nor powers, nor height nor depth, nor anything else in all creation, will be able to separate us from the love of God in Christ Jesus our Lord."

Romans 8:38-39 .

As the day progressed, the doctors came to observe my daughter and they decided to transfer her to intensive care where she would stay for two more months while undergoing rigorous treatments.

I know some people will ask, *"What kind of God is this that would allow people to go through experiences such as these?"*. The answer will come later when God revealed to my husband what was happening in the spiritual realm. The answer from God was the one that healed our hearts and that sustains us until today firmly in His ways loving Him even more now than before.

CHAPTER 8

BE SOBER-MINDED; BE WATCHFUL.

"your adversary the devil prowls around like a roaring lion, seeking someone to devour ."

1 Peter 5:8

Miriam had shown such strength and despite the fact that she spent many nights without sleep, every time I went to visit them, she met me with a smile on her lips. However, one day while our daughter was in intensive care, I went to visit them and found them both very tired. Miriam had a terrible headache and was at the end of her strength to the point that she treated me sharply and Carla did not respond to my affection. Instead she was uncontrollable. She moved from one side to the other and nothing would calm her. It was not the usual reception that I had always received from them. The only thing I could say to them was, *"Let's pray"*.

In the midst of our prayer, I saw two silhouettes lying in the bed next to my child. These figures were of human appearance from head to waist, but they were faceless. From the waist down they were spiral, shaped as a whirlwind. One was electric blue and the other was a fiery red color. I knew that they were demons that had come to torment and to disturb the tranquility of my wife and my daughter. So I immediately took authority over them in the name of Jesus. I ordered them to flee and I saw them dwindle like they were ashamed of being discovered. Finally they disappeared. After this I told my wife that I wanted to leave so that they could rest.

Minutes later Miriam called me by telephone to tell me that her headache had disappeared and that Carla had calmed down and slept peacefully. There were many experiences like this that allowed us to experience dimensions of spiritual warfare that we had never known before.

THE MOMENT OF PASSING

The days passed without any improvement at all. By the end of March, Carla entered yet another crisis and she was paralyzed over the entire left side of her body. My wife suffered terribly. Crying she said, *"Carlos, I can't go any further. I'd rather that Carla go to be with the Lord. I can't go any further"*. I understood, but I responded, *"I will continue fighting for her."* I went to the hospital to stay with her. I prayed, crying and tearing my heart out before the Lord. I read portions of the Bible related to healing. I anointed the room. I anointed her body. I did everything that was at my disposal because as long as I could see her breathe I would not lose hope.

Days later she had another crisis and the doctors didn't know what else they could do to keep her alive. They had tried everything to no avail. They told us that they would start another course of treatment similar to the one they had used for the last 4 months but without any guarantees. It was here that I knew that we could no longer continue like this. Having her there now did not offer any possibility of recovery so we decided to take her home. The doctors accepted and made us sign a waiver releasing them of all responsibility. Science had proven that it could offer nothing more in this case. Only a miracle could change things now.

Little Carla was now two years and two months old and she had a good appetite. We tried to give her as much to eat as possible, but she could not retain what she ate and she would throw it up within a few minutes.

During this particular week we put her to bed in between us to keep her warm, since her little body could not keep warm on its own.

On the morning of April 6 we awoke early. Looking at our little daughter I realized that the time had come. I wrapped her little body in a blanket and took her in my arms. I went to the living room of our apartment and I spoke to my Heavenly Father saying, *"Father, thank you for these two years that you allowed me to enjoy this most beautiful little girl that I have ever known. She is leaving now and I want to commend her into your arms"*. Suddenly I felt the presence of demons and I asked God to remove all evil presence from the house. I experienced in a small way what Jesus must have felt when He gave His life on the cross, when the sky darkened and He said, *"Father, why have you forsaken me?"*

Immediately after that simple prayer, I felt a breeze that cleaned the atmosphere and I continued my prayer, *"Lord, having her has been the most beautiful gift that I have ever received from you. It was my heart's desire that she should live a long time, but clearly it's not going to happen that way, so I want to place her in your hands. Thank you again."* As soon as I finished my prayer, in the midst of my tears, my daughter gave her last breath and went to be with the Lord.

I gathered my courage to tell my wife of her passing. We called our parents and Pastor Alberto Salcedo who worked with me and helped me to make the necessary arrangements. We decided to bury her that same day. Some of the members of the church arrived to be with us. By the afternoon we were taking my little daughter's body to the cemetery. I placed the tiny casket on my lap in Pastor Salcedo's car and before we left, I took a piece of paper and wrote this note:

"My little Carla:

Today I am on my way to bury you. Until today you have been the most precious thing that I have ever had in my life. After today, I no longer live. I will just exist. I don't have the will to continue living. There is nothing left in life that interests me. Today I bury my heart with you.

Your Daddy"

There was no hearse and no flowers. We only had the company of family and a few friends from church. These friends had been with us through the most difficult times.

When a person loses a father we call him, "orphan". When a person loses a spouse, we call them "widow" or "widower". When a person loses a son or a daughter, there is no name by which to call them. There is no name for that. It is not natural because one would expect the children to bury the parents and not vice versa and here we were burying our daughter, the treasure of my life. It was the most difficult moment of my life. I was burying what I loved the most.

We arrived at the cemetery and the brothers in Christ began to worship our God. When the workers finished placing the headstone, they let me inscribe on it,

"...Let the children come to me; do not hinder them for to such belongs the kingdom of God."

Mark 10:14

We left the cemetery knowing that we were beginning a new stage in our lives as a couple, as a family and as ministers of the gospel. We had our eldest son, Jose, who seemed not to understand what was happening. We did not know how we would face the days ahead; the only thing left was to give our utmost to God in prayer,

"Lord, I don't understand what has happened. You know I love you.

I have left everything for you, my hopes and my dreams. I have given them up to give all of me to you.

I have served you since I was young. I cannot depart from you because there is no other God aside from you.

I know you too well to leave the ministry now, but the pain in my heart is too great. The only thing I ask is that when I am ready that you will help me to understand what has happened because I really don't understand it."

I had lost the only treasure that I considered truly mine in this life. I let my tears run freely for awhile. Only one question kept going through my mind: *"What happened?!"*

CHAPTER 9

HIDE NOT YOUR FACE FROM YOUR SERVANT;

"for I am in distress; make haste to answer me."

Psalm 69:17

Why...?This question went through my head over and over again a thousand times without receiving a rational answer from God. I was very sad, but I kept preaching. The pain had attached itself to my heart, but I kept waiting for an answer. The ministry kept growing. The Lord used me as an instrument so that many people were healed. Before my very eyes passed many people who were moved and transformed by the power of God…but I was still asking, *"Why couldn't a miracle have been done for my daughter?"*

Two days after Carla died a mother arrived with her *son* who was the same age as Carla. The child was plagued with the same repeated diarrhea, the same symptoms that had claimed the life of Carla. I felt furious and I released him of that sickness saying, "In *the name of Jesus, whatever illness you might be, leave the body of this child!"* One week later the mother of the child called me very happy and emotional to tell me that her son was totally healed after that prayer and that he was eating without any problems. Again I insisted before God, "*Lord, do you not understand? Father…I prayed to you many times for my daughter. I fasted; I convened a fast of the church members throughout the world so that they would intercede. I did so many things so see my daughter healed and nonetheless she died…now this lady comes with her son having the very same sickness. I prayed only one time and you healed him! I don't understand! I don't understand, Lord! When I needed you, where was the God of miracles that I have known and whose word I have preached? Where was the God of power that I had seen work in my church? Lord, I just simply don't understand! Speak to me!"*

This was my prayer for one year. Every time I began to seek God to prepare a message, I cried for 2 hours first and then I would always end the same way, *"I don't understand!"*

"There was a man in the land of Uz, whose name was Job; and that man was blameless and upright, one who feared God, and turned away from evil."

Job 1:1

After an extremely long year I was invited to Brazil to give a leaders seminar in a church in the city of Uberlandia. Once there, the pastor of that church, Harry Scates and I were invited to the home of a Peruvian lady whose husband had experienced great suffering as the result of a terrible accident. Sitting at the table, she asked the pastor a question, *"Pastor...why do we Christians suffer?"* Before he said anything, he turned to me, *"Do you know why Christians suffer?"* *I could only answer, "I have an idea..."*

The pastor says to us, *"Have you read the book of Job?"* In that moment I heard a voice on my left side. It was the Holy Spirit of God who said to me, *"Listen. This is the answer that you have been waiting for this past year."*

I paid very close attention so I could hear everything that the Lord spoke by way of this pastor. When he finished speaking, I had learned a lesson on faith that restored my soul and healed the pain that tormented me day after day; a lesson that we want to share with everybody, especially those who have passed through similar experiences and who are also asking God questions.

" And the LORD said to Satan, "Have you considered my servant Job, that there is none like him on the earth, a blameless and upright man, who fears God and turns away from evil?" Then Satan answered the LORD and said, "Does job fear God for no reason? Have You not put a hedge around him and his whole house and all that he has. on every side? You have blessed the work of his hands, and his possessions have increased in the land. But stretched out your hand and touch all that he has, and he will curse you to your face." And the LORD said to Satan, "Behold, all that he has is in your hand. Only against him do not stretch out your hand." So Satan went out from the presence of the LORD."

Job 1:8-12

The Bible describes Job as a just man, obedient to God, abundantly blessed, father of many sons and daughters and a very, very rich man. This man took great pains to live in holiness every day before God and to this end he purified himself and prayed for his family.

Satan thinks that we Christians love and serve God because of what He gives us. Job lost all his possessions, his sons and his daughters and when Satan was waiting for Job to stop loving God, the answer came:

"...Naked I came from my mother's womb, and naked shall I return. The LORD gave, and the LORD has taken away; blessed be

the name of the LORD"

Job 1:21

Satan also took away his health, but every time he took something from him, Job continued to be faithful to God.

Job's wife, seeing that her husband's flesh was infested with worms, scorned him and renouncing God as unjust, spoke to her husband saying: *"Then his wife said to him, "Do you still hold fast your integrity? Curse God and die."* (*Job 2:9*) And Job answered, *"...But he said to her, "You speak as one of the foolish women would speak. Shall we receive good from God, and shall we not receive evil?" In all this Job did not sin with his lips."* (*Job 2:10*)

Nonetheless, God had a reward for the faith and integrity of Job. After all these experiences, the Lord restored everything to him, he lifted him up, and he healed him. He gave him twice what he previoulsy had. He also gave him children and again Job was a prosperous man according to the Word and in all areas of his life.

HAVE YOU SEEN MY SERVANT...?

Many times it looks like Christians suffer for no reason at all, but the reason for our suffering is really declared in the heavens. Satan, our accuser, wants to show God that we only serve Him for the blessings He bestows on us and that when He withdraws them that we will abandon Him quickly. The reality, however, is that because God is "proud" of us he challenges Satan, *"Have you seen my servant... (place your name here)...see how perfect he is and how he fears God and separates himself from evil?"*

I dropped my jaw, appropriating every word that the pastor explained, but despite this I still couldn't completely understand how this explanation was the response to the cry of my heart.

When I arrived at the place where I was staying, I said to God, "*Lord this teaching was very nice. I learned a great lesson regarding faith and integrity but...What does this have to do with what has happened in my life?*

This was when the presence of God flooded the room and I heard the Lord say to me, ***"I want you to know that the devil came to me one day and I asked him, 'Have you seen my servant, Carlos?' and he responded that he had. I continued saying, 'Have you seen how he serves me since his youth and that he has given up everything for me?' and again the devil responded in the affirmative. Satan then challenged me to prove your integrity and your faithfulness toward me saying, 'Take away what he most loves and you will see how he will forsake you and how he will abandon you! And I told him, 'Alright, touch what he loves the most.'"***

There I began to understand. The answer gained clarity in my heart. The adversary had challenged God like he did with Job. The devil descended and touched my daughter, made her sick and took her life.

Later the Lord spoke to me and He said, ***"Carlos, I knew that you would not leave me, that you would not abandon the faith or the service of my ministry. I have trusted you, and I want you to know that the death of your daughter was***

not a loss, but an offering to me, because that is how I have received it".

Then the words of the Brazilian prophet that God had used long before Little Carla went home to the Lord returned to me. Carla was the great offering that I had given over to the Lord...the sacrifice offering.

As soon as I heard His voice, my heart was healed. I was filled with the peace of the Lord. My mourning was changed into praise and joy, having found the answer where there was none before. Receiving comfort for that which is inconsolable and making sense of what is humanly impossible to explain. Still a new question came to mind, *"How could God have trusted so much in me, a simple human being.* And the Spirit responded, **"God trusts you. He knew that you would not leave him or abandon Him".**

Not only was I healed of that terrible wound, but I was profoundly honored that God trusted in us to such an extent, even knowing our weaknesses and the frailty of our hearts. This experience opened the doors to another dimension of complete intimacy with God and I understood perfectly the verse in *Romans 8:39, "nor height nor depth, nor anything else in all creation, will be able to separate us from the love of God in Christ Jesus our Lord.*

I returned to Bolivia with a whole new understanding and motivation, grateful and profoundly impressed with the revelation I had received and I poured out this balm of restoration over Miriam who, upon hearing these words, tearfully received the same healing. The faithfulness and love of God were newly confirmed in our lives.

"These all died in faith, not having received the things promised, but having seen them and greeted them from afar, and having acknowledged that they were strangers and exiles on the earth."

Hebrews 11:13

I shared about our healing in a message to the congregation that by that time had grown to several thousand.

Many times we think that something is already over, but God has ways of demonstrating to us that there is a lot more race to be run. He doesn't do things halfway and He has different ways of finishing a work and generally it is not how we imagine it but simply a way that will glorify Him in a very specific way.

Miriam and I thought that we had already lived a sufficiently difficult experience but we still had to comprehend what was happening with the health of Jose. Because of this we decided not to have any more children and to dedicate ourselves completely to the work of the Lord. We mentioned this decision to Jose's pediatrician in one of our visits and he encouraged us to reconsider. He argued that we were still young and we had a full life ahead of us. In any case we decided to wait as long as we could to make the decision about having another child, but since God is in charge and governs by His will, on the 16th of August of 1989, Sara Stephanie arrived.

I had hoped to feel really happy at her coming since she was such a precious little girl, a reflection of her mother, but for some reason, in my heart was a tremendous uncertainty. I was afraid to get attached to her like I had to Carla. I was confused. I had to occupy myself with the care of our children, serve as pastor to thousands of people with divergent needs, travel all around the country planting new churches to fulfill the vision of our church that was growing every day and in addition, I had to make time to visit new medical specialists that worked to figure out the problems now troubling Jose, our eldest son.

Without planning or much preparation, in 1991 we awaited still another new arrival. During this time God was speaking to us a great deal about Daniel in the Bible. It was so strong that we believed that our last child would be a boy, but on May 3rd God gave us another daughter, Paula Daniela. We had 3 beautiful children! Our quiver was full. Our joy was complete.

By this time the church had 12,000 members. We owned the "Sistema Cristiano de Comunicaciones" (Christian Communications System), a radio frequency that reached all of the city and the surrounding towns as well as a television channel that transmitted to 52 Spanish-speaking cities all over the continent. Newspapers and magazines dedicated entire pages to cover our ministry and "Carisma" (Charisma) magazine put out an elaborate article about our church publishing it in English which gave us international exposure. We were considered extremely successful pastors. During two consecutive years, we received recognition from "Enfoques" ("Focus") magazine as most outstanding people in the nation. The church was living some glorious moments that everyone enjoyed. Definitely, the Lord was with us! We were sure that the time of hardship was over.

CHAPTER 10

JOSE

"Therefore do not throw away your confidence, which has a great reward. For you have need of endurance, so that when you have done the will of God you may receive what is promised."

Hebrews 10: 35, 36

We had somewhat forgotten about our Little Jose during the time of tribulation over the loss of Little Carla.

When Jose was 3 years old he could not walk without stumbling or falling and due to his problems with balance and low muscle tone, the pediatrician recommended that he receive a program of integrated therapies to prepare him for school and his future.

We decided to dedicate ourselves to his care and to this end we acquired the services of neurologists, pediatricians, psychologists and specialists who had trained in foreign countries and doctors of a certain reputation and prestige in the city. We got different diagnoses from each of them which only confused us. Some said the problems were due to birth injuries.

When Jose was two years old, we were at home and I was playing the guitar and praising the Lord with my wife. Suddenly, Jose sat in a big chair in front of us and we felt a grand and marvelous presence of the Lord. Jose's face shined and noticed an expression of adoration that confirmed how the Lord was touching him. He raised his hands and tried to sing the songs like we did. I knew right then that our son was being touched by the Holy Spirit of God.

A NEW BATTLE BEGINS: AS TOLD BY MIRIAM

As a mother, I admired my son, Jose, when he demonstrated his abilities. When he was 3 years old his father taught him how to differentiate distinct models of cars by the sound of their engines and he could distinguish a car, a truck and other types of motor vehicles. We knew there was nothing wrong with his intellect.

We found a particular institute where a psychologist friend of mine gave him motor skills therapy and she concluded that in fact his intellect was developing normally. Jose went to therapy from 10 a.m. to 12 p.m., three times a week and despite the difficulty involved, he enjoyed it very much. Since it was relatively close to home, we loved to walk the seven long blocks to get there. Jose was very observant and always asked a lot of questions.

He received physical and psychological theraphy, as well as his academic lessons. His progress reports were encouraging. Obviously he didn't walk like the other children, neither could he run, but his academic performance was normal.

By age 5, Jose had a fight with one of his little friends and he came home crying from school. I was touched and I explained to him that he was not alone, that besides his parents he could always count on the company of Jesus. I told him that he could have Him close to protect him and keep him safe from all evil if he would accept Him into his heart. In that moment Jose understood the message and decided to give his life to Jesus

Christ. From that moment on, he felt secure and he was happy to go to classes after I prayed with him. He was an extremely tender and affectionate child.

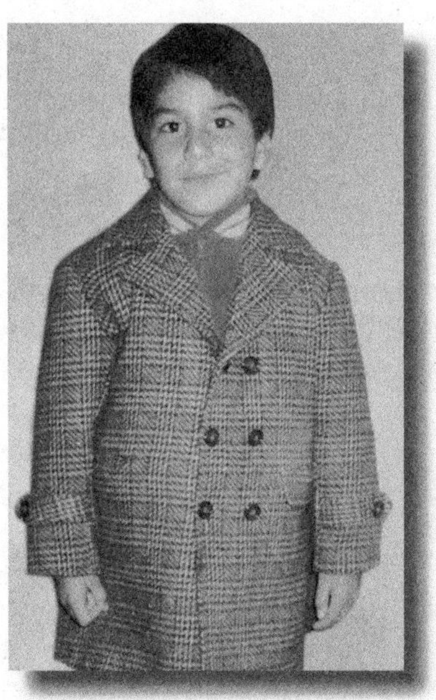

Jose Esteban, 5 years old. La Paz Bolivia

At six years old he entered elementary school and the first year was the best year of his life because he had an exceptional teacher who was also a pediatrician. Doctor Liliana Beltran was able to help him maximize his academic potential and she also supervised and took his physical condition into account. Doctor Beltran could make the other children be aware of Jose and considerate of his condition. She did this by allowing him certain privileges like being the first to go out for recess and the first to go to the restroom if he needed it. She would concern herself about his eating his breakfast, and when he couldn't do it, she would help him. God bless those kinds of merciful people!

The next 2 years were harder due to our son's difficulty in walking. It was difficult for him to button his shirt or to zip up his pants. He had difficulty holding his pencil and it was very difficult for him to write.

Jose participated in all the school's outdoor activities like the rest of the kids, but since he couldn't run, during sports time they always sat him down to watch the others. That year we all suffered when he had second degree burns in his arms, his face and his skin. This is how we discovered that Jose was extremely sensitive to the sun. For 15 days he had to subject himself to a course of treatment so rigorous that he had to avoid even one ray of sunshine for several days. His room had to be completely covered and dark. He could not play outside or go out. He couldn't even go to the living room because through the windows the sunlight would filter in. This was a very difficult thing for a small boy to understand, but when he received the logical explanations and the medical reasons relative to his condition, he understood and simply obeyed. Jose's attitude was admirable.

I would melt with sadness and I didn't know what to do for him. It hurt me to think of the limitations he had in school like how much shame and frustration he might experience because he couldn't do what the others did or the mocking of the children when he would have an accident not making it to the bathroom in time or when he was unable to deal with the zipping up of his pants.

I would see him limited to his classroom, just looking out the window watching his friends racing and playing games. But his mind was set on learning more, so I had to make a decision. We got someone to take care of our daughters and I asked for permission to attend school with Jose. I would be his hands and his feet. I would read his lessons. I would take his exams and write his answers down for him with all honesty. I would do everything that was necessary to help him continue absorbing all the knowledge that he could. There was no one happier than Jose. He felt protected and loved.

He loved animals and enjoyed watching television programs about wildlife. One day his father took him to a pet store and they returned with a few little fish. Little by little they kept buying a few at a time until they had 50 of different colors and sizes. His father would read to him about fish, and studying his fish tank he learned the characteristics of each kind of fish. His friends were amazed when he described the details of each fish and he gave them so much love that some of them also began to keep a fish tank of their own.

Jose also had some parakeets, white lab mice, two sea turtles, and a dog. To top it off, he had a parrot that called out saying, *"Pastor! Pastor!"* We thought that he would grow up to be a veterinarian or a chef because he also loved international cooking shows on television.

At 10 years of age a severe pulmonary infection overtook him. He coughed so badly it would cause him difficulty breathing and we had to hospitalize him with pleurisy. To save his life they placed a catheter directly into his lung without the benefit of anesthesia. He was in the hospital for one week on very strong antibiotics and this provided the opportunity for him to reaffirm his faith in Jesus.

His low muscle tone was increasing and he was not able to walk by himself. For this reason, the following year, he was home schooled by a private teacher.

Jose did not complain. He would accept his limitations with patience. He had a very sweet expresion in his eyes that would cause his dad to call him "mi mapachito" (my little racoon).

He was very loving and he always had a smile in his lips although he was ill and weak. Jose would fill my life with joy and he would multiply my strengh everyday to continue moving forward.

God gave me supernatural fortitude throughtout this time, given that in the midst of these circumstances our two other daughters also began to show symptoms of a deteriorating health. Jose's health worsened and in my husband a question arose "Lord, what is happening?"

Some believed that it was a contradiction to see my husband preaching the gospel and praying for the sick that would receive healing, but our children continued ill, but despite it all the church continued growing.

CHAPTER 11

SARA: SENT TO COMFORT

"For as we share abundantly in Christ's sufferings, so through Christ we share abundantly in comfort too."

2 Corinthians 1: 5

Little Sara was happy by my side. It was obvious that she loved me immensely. She sought out any opportunity to accompany me and play with me. Everything I would say had an absolute value to her.

One day, my wife and I heard the girls having a conversation regarding a soap opera on television. Their maternal grandmother liked soap operas and she would watch them while she cared for our daughters. So I had given the instruction that they were not to watch television unless I allowed it so that the girls would not be influenced by those programs.

The next day, when my mother-in-law turned on the television to see her favorite soap opera, Little Sara stood in front of the television set so her grandmother could not watch the program. My mother-in-law said that Sara declared, *"My father said that the television could not be watched!"* She spoke so vehemently that the television had to be turned off.

Our daughter loved music. She was a very healthy child who sang all day long. One day her maternal grandmother heard her singing, *"…I am in love with my mannnn…."* And immediately she told Miriam because it seemed strange that Little Sara would sing such lyrics so inappropriate for a child her age. Miriam asked her what the song was about. Sara explained that the song was about Jesus!

THE RED BLANKIE

One day as I arrived from church, I heard a commotion. My mother-in-law, Jose , Daniela and our live-in nanny were observing Sara and my wife deal with a situation regarding Sara's little red blanket.

Miriam had arrived from running errands to find Little Sara bawling her eyes out. She wanted to take her nap and sleep with her "blankie", her red "blankie"! No one could find her red blanket. Finally Miriam said, "*Show me which one is your red blanket?"* Then little Sara pointed to a yellow blanket that my mother-in-law had lovingly knitted for her. Carefully, Miriam placed her in her bed and explained, "*My little one, this is not a red blanket. It's yellow."* Sara replied, "*No, mommy, this is my red blanket.* Again and again Miriam tried to show her the difference between the colors, but she had no success at all. This made the child cry even more and Miriam was losing control of the situation when I came in.

After hearing the explanation from my wife, everyone was now looking at me. They expected me to correct Sara. Then little Sara asked the million dollar question, *"Papi…can't you see that my blanket is red?"*

By this time, my mother-in-law was staring at me, the nanny's face had turned red due to nervousness and Jose, standing in front of us, looked confused as to what was going on. Sarita waited looking at me like she knew my answer would give her the assurance that she needed.

Then in a moment of suspense, I said, *"For everyone in this house, from this day on, this blanket is 'Sarita's red blanket!'"*.

My mother-in-law could not believe what she was hearing. The nanny laughed nervously and Miriam wanted to eat me alive with her gaze. Then Sarita turned to her mother and said, *"See, mommy? This is my red blanket. My Papi said so"*.

Later I had to explain to my wife that the child was too young to learn her colors and until she was old enough to understand we just had to be patient with her.

Sarita went with me to the racquetball courts where she watched me play while she played with her dolls and waited to go home with me. She would be so happy just to sit on my lap. Sara was the only one who accompanied me as I ministered.

Once I had a commitment to preach an Easter service in the city of Cochabamba. It was a very important service. Thousands of people would be there in the city coliseum. Miriam could not take care of her because she was busy caring for Daniela who had been hospitalized with an infection.

Jose was being cared for by my mother-in-law, but Sara didn't want to stay with them. We agreed that she would go with me.

It was the most exciting adventure of her life, travelling with her father, sleeping in the same room and to have me all to herself the whole time that I wasn't preaching. This was the best thing that could happen to Sara.

I couldn't understand all this love from my child. Despite the fact that my heart was healed over the loss of Carla, somehow I just couldn't accept this great love from my Sarita. I only made time for her when it was necessary. So many times she would affectionately get close to me, but I would refer her to her mother.

One day I was confronted about my attitude. I remember that Miriam asked me why I didn't love Sara the same way that I had loved Carla. I had no answer, but later having meditated on this matter, the answer I came up with scared me. There were still some things in me that needed the touch of God. I didn't want to love anyone again because it just seemed like everything I loved died. Obviously, it was related to Carla.

I was surprised to have found this so deeply imbedded in my heart and that this had become an impediment to my enjoying the pure love of my innocent little daughter. She really should not have been named Sara Stephanie, but Sara "Consuelo" (Comforter) because then I understood that she was sent by God to console and bring healing to the deep wound that my heart had endured. I now understood what had happened with Carla, but there had been something else, my deepest feelings, those that I even didn't understand. They needed to be healed and God, who sees everything, recognized them and sent me a daughter whose mission in life was to heal the heart of her father. Little Sara achieved that goal a few years later.

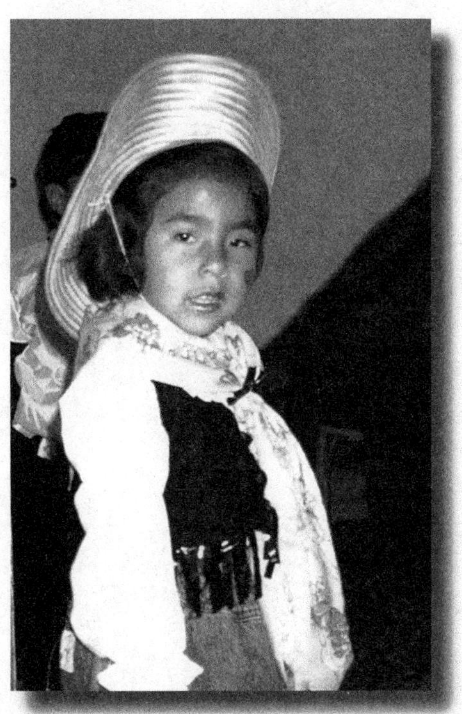

Sarita in Elementary School at the age of 5

CHAPTER 12

DANIELA: THE CHILD OF UNITY

"To grant to those who mourn in Zion— to give them a beautiful headdress instead of ashes, the oil of gladness instead of mourning, the garment of praise instead of a faint spirit;..."

Isaiah 61:3a

Paula Daniela proved to be a joyful child, she was dynamic, diligent and cooperative. She had a very defined personality and a strong and unbending character. Sometimes she would have to be disciplined more than once and later when I would ask, *"Have you repented?"*, many times she would respond *"No!"*. We never let our children see discipline as synonymous with rejection; so that once the problem was rectified, we would show them a lot of affection. She would respond in a marvelous manner changing into an obedient and docile child.

On my book shelf, Miriam would keep the coloring books. Once when she was gone to a women's activity at the church, I stayed home to take care of the children. Jose was quiet and contented to watch his favorite program on television on international cuisine. Daniela and Sara asked me for the coloring books, but I couldn't find them. Then Daniela with a jolt of sarcasm (genetically inherited I'm sure), says, "Are you dumb?"

Miriam arrived in that moment while I was still surprised by my daughter's reaction. Miriam didn't know what to say. I decided to be gracious. I looked straight back at her and said jokingly, *"I am one of the most respected pastors in the country, recognized throughout the continent, hundreds of leaders follow my instructions and millions of people watch me on television…and you insult me this way?!"* She smiled and with a satisfied look, she took the coloring books that her mother had handed to her and marched off with her sister Sara without any further comment.

Despite our past experiences, God had given us the blessings and joys of being a family with many beautiful moments. Miriam worked hard at being a loving mother and a selfless wife although her desire to serve in the church would not go away. We felt that we would have a chance to work together in the ministry once the children were grown…

Miriam and 5 year old Daniela. Virginia, USA

CHAPTER 13

IMUNODEFICIENCY

In general the health of the children was good. Nevertheless we noticed certain characteristics that seemed unusual, but we didn't realize the extent of the problem. This happened with their colds, for example, which became troubling. Daniela had a particularly difficult time overcoming them and Jose had started to suffer a cough that later became chronic and kept him on antibiotics and in physical therapy. We would do pretty much everything that was at our disposal to solve these problems.

Sara was the healthiest of the three and had an excellent appetite just like Daniela. She had hardly been sick until the day when she was 3 that she awoke with a significant and suspicious inflammation on one of her fingers. When Miriam showed me her hand, I took her to the doctor thinking that she had dislocated or broken it as the extent of the inflammation seemed to indicate these possibilities.

Later the X-rays showed that there was nothing wrong with her bones, but no one could explain the inflammation on her finger. She wasn't complaining about any pain, so we had no alternative but to wait and see.

At the same time, Daniela came down with a cold that quickly turned into bronchitis. She ended up hospitalized for three days since the standard treatments had no effect.

By now we were on a mission to find out what was threatening the health of our children. The fact that we had such a large congregation allowed us to have contact with many people of various professions who wanted to help us. Among them was a European-trained specialist who offered to run some blood tests on the children. Thanks to her we discovered that our children had a strange abnormality in their immune system. Sara had almost none of two particular immunoglobulin characteristics, but she had another one in excess and this protected her against infections which explained why she didn't get sick very much. The immunoglobulin for Jose was normal but his respiratory problems were not getting solved. Daniela's levels, on the other hand, were very low, almost nonexistent.

When Daniela was hospitalized for bronchitis, we were able to count on our health insurance covering the cost of treatment and hospitalization. Our finances had improved and that gave us the ability to seek out better assistance for our children.

FACING DEATH

After those three days of treatments in the hospital, Daniela was released. Two days later when she came home, she got a very high fever during the night. The next day when Miriam changed her diaper, she noticed a blotch on Daniela's stomach that looked rather strange, but that I didn't pay much attention to. I told her to let me know if there were any changes. By mid-day Daniela was in shock, the blotch was much larger and it covered a good part of her stomach. We took her to the emergency room on the advice of her pediatrician. This doctor, who was a very stoic person, examined her and noticed other similar blotches on the back of her left leg and on her heel and he looked very worried. He wrote a very long report and he told us that she had a very serious condition and to prepare ourselves for the worst. We had to hospitalize her immediately in a private hospital that would examine her and give her emergency treatment.

By nightfall they gave us the news: Daniela was suffering from sepsis, a powerful infection that had overtaken her bodily defenses and entered her blood stream. We knew that a diagnosis like this meant a patient was at the point of death.

We didn't know what to do and uncertainty flooded our thoughts. The shadow of death was present again. My spiritual senses were sharpened, my emotions were completely supressed and I prayed with all my strength. When something serious happened with my children, my entire being went into battle. I was converted into a decision-making machine ready to do the impossible to solve the problem.

The doctor feared that the infection had entered her bones. The trauma specialist tapped her spine to examine the fluid. A chilling fear flooded the hospital room and we were tormented by an unknown enemy that we were facing and the victim was the tiniest of our daughters. Daniela was only 20 months old.

THE DIAGNOSIS

Our little Daniela had needles in her arms and feet through which they gave her fluids and antibiotics. She was swollen and by then the lab cultures had identified the bacteria that was responsible for the damage to Daniela's body. It was pseudomonas aeruginosa, a bacterium so aggressive that in a matter of hours (just like it did) it could produce sepsis and then death. This type of bacteria is also found in hospitals and they are extremely resistant to even the strongest antibiotics.

In order to explain the nature of the bacteria, the doctor

told us, *"It's as though your daughter had an open wound and was then placed in the dirtiest latrine."* Our daughter had contracted this during her three-day stay in the hospital for bronchitis. Knowing that Daniela's immune system was compromised, the pediatrician requested 15 vials of an antibiotic that was not only expensive, but difficult to obtain. We went to countless pharmacies looking for the medication, until someone found a doctor who had 2 vials which he offered to us on the condition that we replace them. One of our brothers in Christ had a relative who was in the business of importing medications. This blessed brother checked all the pharmacies in the country and finally found the rest of the vials. God bless all the angels of flesh and blood who helped us in so many ways during our painful pilgrimage. We owe them a love debt that we can never repay.

While we were in this process, friends and acquaintances in their zeal to help us, suggested that we move the child to another hospital and that we should find another specialist because we were not seeing any results from the treatments of the pediatrician. This confused me greatly and on top of all the pressure I was experiencing already, I had to decide whether to change doctors and hospitals or continue as we were. Faced with this situation, I prayed desperately, *"My God, help me. I don't know what to do!"* I opened the Bible because my mind could not hear the voice of God. I read the verse that said,

"Be patient, therefore, brothers, until the coming of the Lord. See how the farmer waits for the precious fruit of the earth, being patient about it, until it receives the early and the late rains"

James 5:7

Then I understood that God wanted to wait for the fruit of the treatment. It is so important to recognize that we have recourse in prayer and to know that God responds in the most difficult of circumstances.

The bacteria advanced to her leg, her calf and her heel and caused a huge wound in her stomach. The pediatrician said that the infection had to be removed surgically to remove the dead flesh. Daniela had to fast until the surgery which meant she would have to go long hours without food. Miriam would sing to her, pray for her and even promise her she could eat anything she wanted after the surgery, but nothing worked until Miriam decided to give her a piece of chewing gum. Such a wise decision! Daniela chewed the gum before going into surgery; she prayed with her mother and asked for the company of angels. She was off to surgery with a smile and waving her little hands as she entered the operating room. She was operated on a total of 10 times.

On one of those occasions a particular surgical nurse was assigned to assist in the operating room. She had a stellar record of impeccable performance in the operating room that spanned a 15 year period. Upon seeing the wound on our daughter she exclaimed, *"My God, what sin did the parents of this child commit that she should have such a horrible open wound!!"* At that moment the scalpel that she was passing to the surgeon "slipped" from her hands causing a gash in the palm of her hand. The scalpel fell on the open wound of my daughter without causing any harm. Startled by this, the nurse reflexively reached out with her wounded hand and the blood from my daughter's open wound mixed with her own exposing her to the possibility of contracting the dangerous bacterium. She had to leave the operating room immediately and seek medical attention including painful intramuscular injections for a period of 15 days. Later she discovered that the parents of this child were Christian pastors and she became very afraid confessing, "I will never again say anything against a Christian!"

THE EXPERIENCE WITH GOD

Daniela had spent 4 months in the hospital. Miriam had converted that room into a prayer altar. She always hoped that our little girl was asleep when she poured out her heart before the Lord. She had purposed to encourage Daniela with her sweet words, her faith, her joy and her smile. We wanted our little girl to feel secure and not see her mother in tears.

On one particular occasion Miriam was unaware that Daniela had awakened and that she was watching her crying on her knees in her room. Miriam heard her small voice say, "Mama, why are you crying?" A surprised Miriam could only say, "Well, I'm praying for you asking Jesus to heal you." Miriam asked Daniela if she wanted to invite Jesus into her heart. Daniela accepted the invitation and her mother led her through a brief prayer. Afterwards Daniela said, "Pass me the 'lible' (Bible)". For several minutes she leafed through her Bible acting as though she were reading it. She was 2 years old and her attitude of reverence and love were already evident whenever we prayed or sang in the name of Jesus.

RETURN OF THE INFECTION

Daniela's condition was a roller coaster ride. Good news made us happy one day only to be dashed with a new crisis the next.

When the worst seemed to have passed, Daniela had a fever. The doctors did a blood test to find out the cause and after a few days they returned with the news. The infection had returned. It was the first time I saw her pediatrician resigned to the situation and without a plan to fight for her. Since he was not very communicative, he left and returned with a prescription in his hand. When he handed it to me he said, *"This medication is very difficult to find. If you can find it at all it is the only thing that will save your daughter. If you cannot find it, there is nothing we can do."* The medication was unknown in the pharmacies and our friends in the import business did not know where to find it either.

"How is little Daniela?" It was Graciela Vasquez, a friend who attended our church and who worked at the American embassy. I told her about the medicine that was impossible to find. She asked me to show her the prescription and within a few days she appeared with a package in hand which contained the necessary injections. After I thanked her I asked how much it cost and she said, *"Pastor, don't worry. They are already paid for."*

The angels that make up the body of Christ are marvelous. The children of God are as soothing oil to a suffering heart.

I arrived at the hospital with the medication in hand and gave it to the doctor who looked at me with utter surprise and asked, *"How did you get it?" You surprise me! This is incredible!"* It was an example of how God was providing for us. It was as though He was saying, *"Daniela will not die for lack of medication. She will come to me in her proper time."* Daniela received the treatments for 10 days and during all this we continued our ministerial commitments. During this time we held a concert with a very famous singer and I was to serve as master of ceremonies. While the concert continued my heart was elsewhere, with my daughter in the hospital.

The wounds on my daughter's body were so large and deep like third degree burns that festered for a long time. They had consumed so much of her skin and flesh that finally her plastic surgeon decided to act aggressively because he no longer held out hope that she would survive. In addition to her gangrenous tissue, he also took some of her healthy tissue and grafted freeze-dried pig tissue that was especially treated to kill any existing bacteria. This was done to assist in regenerating the cells of her own skin.

After this surgery, Daniela was subjected to several minor surgical procedures and treatments in the operating room to clean her wounds.

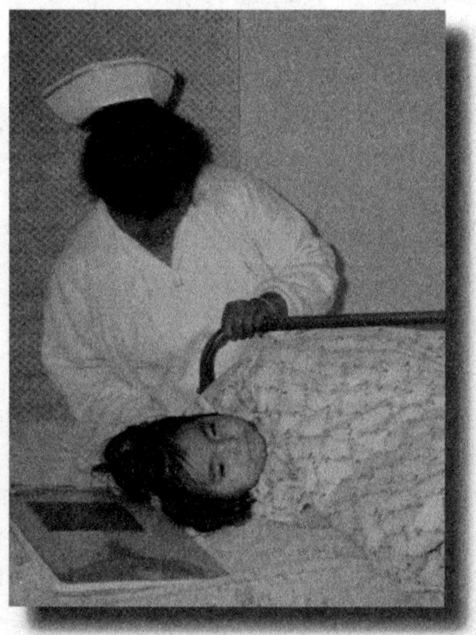

Daniela in one of the 10 times that she entered the operating room. (Clinica de la Caja Petrolera, La Paz, Bolivia)

Just when we thought that Daniela was out of danger, the doctor discovered in her pre-release exam, that she had some abscesses in her knee, another under her navel and another in her groin area. Visibly shaken he said, "If these abscesses that are visible on the outside are also on the inside, there is nothing we can do. We are going to drain them, then run some tests and wait." This is when Miriam and I entered into the most difficult moment of the experience. Only God could free our daughter. We prayed, *"Lord, up to this point we have done everything within our power for our daughter, now we give her to you to do your will."*

Daniela was not doing well. The doctors drained the three abscesses. They disinfected them. We had to wait three days.

On the morning of the fourth day, the plastic surgeon entered the room, looked at our daughter who was bandaged from head to toe; he cut off all the bandages, examined her and lifted up her little naked body handing her over to Miriam declaring, "Madam, your daughter is without infection. Take her as far away from this hospital as possible. We don't want her to get infected again".

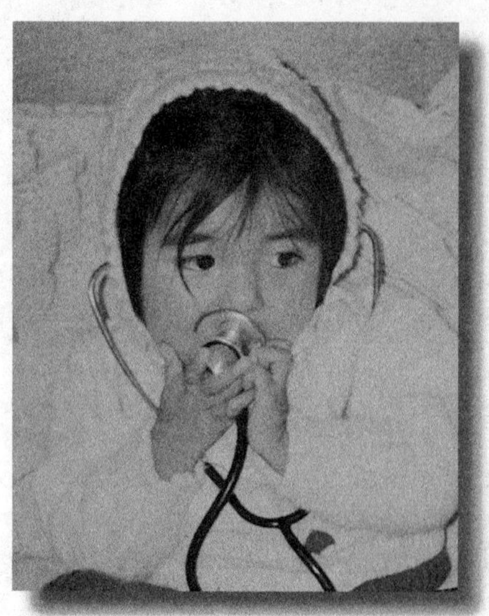

Daniela is released after 4 months in the hospital

He recommended that we expose her to the fresh outdoors and that she should be around nature so that her little body could strengthen her immunological system.

After dressing our little daughter, I remember that Miriam came to tell me that we could go home. Looking into the eyes of my daughter, I prayed authoritatively speaking to the spirit of death saying, *"We have conquered you. You didn't beat us this time. Victory is ours in Jesus' name."*

"Death is swallowed up in victory." "O death, where is your victory? O death, where is your sting?"

I Corinthians 15: 54b-55

By this time God had given us a car through one of the members of the church. We left the hospital and headed for the closest ice cream shop to buy ice cream. We rode around with our little Daniela who was beside herself because she was dressed and sitting on her mother's lap enjoying her frozen treat. This was just short of paradise for her after those long four months in bed.

We fully enjoyed those simple moments that we often trivialize and take for granted when we are in good health. We learned to value the most simple moments and to enjoy the tiniest things as a gift from God

Daniela from her return from the hospital hugged by her sister

CHAPTER 14

FACING THE INCOMPREHENSIBLE

About six months had passed since those days in which Daniela had been healed. By now the church knew that something unusual was happening with the health of our children. Some of the members of the church showed us their sympathy in so many ways, others prayed for our family; still others just quietly loved us, but that love covered us with a hedge of protection.

Among the thousands of helpers at the church, there was one very special person. Her name was Lourdes Ursic who suffered from multiple myeloma, a terminal condition. Nonetheless, she was a fighter who loved the Lord and she trusted in His power. Lourdes was preparing to travel to the United States and she came to say goodbye to a friend whom we were visiting. When she saw me helping my son walk, she said, *"Pastor, I promise you that I will do everything that I can so that your children can go to the same hospital to which I am going."* Somewhat skeptical I thanked her for her offer, not knowing whether that would ever happen, but her love was evident and that was the most important thing to us.

A few days later we received a call from the United States. Lourdes had championed our cause in detail and was informing us that there were doctors who were offering diagnostic assistance. We only had a few weeks to prepare, gather the necessary funds and depart. We had no idea where we would stay or how much it would cost for transportation. There just wasn't enough time to consider all these things.

In September of 1994 we landed at Reagan National Airport in Washington, DC. This huge vehicle awaited us. The driver was the son-in-law of a sister in Christ in whose home we were to stay. We were two families living under the same roof along with the grandmother of the family, Carmen Albarracin, who was another one of our flesh and blood angels. She was one of the 12,000 members of Ekklesia in Bolivia and she had been praying that her children would receive us in their home. In the days that followed we were joined by several members of our church who had emigrated to the north. As always, we were once again able to experience God's faithfulness in every detail.

THE TRUTH IN THE UNITED STATES

In 1994 Jose was 10 years old, Sarita was 5 and Daniela was 2. Lourdes had written letters in English and was able to get us an appointment with a pediatrician who had to see us before the National Institutes of Health (NIH) would consider our case. The doctor met us accompanied by an assistant. They listened for an hour to all the details of our children's ailments. They asked us to wait while they deliberated and they returned about a half hour later with good news and bad news.

We asked for the good news first: they had identified the cause of all of our childrens' health problems. We had waited 10 years to get a proper diagnosis. The doctor said, *"We are 95% sure of what's troubling your children. We will need to run some blood tests and some images to be able to confirm 100%."*

Then they told us the name of the disease: **ATAXIA TELANGIECTASIA.** It was due to a recessive gene. If we had each married someone else, it would not have manifested, but both Miriam and I were carriers of that gene which made it dominant. This illness caused degenerative neurological deficiencies and also affected various systems of the body in different ways. Sometimes it would attack the digestive system, like had happened with Carlita, and in many cases it completely compromised the immune system which was true for Sara and Daniela, or it would impede normal muscular development. In addition, it produced problems with equilibrium, the respiratory system and affected muscle tone. Persons affected by the disease generally end up in a wheel chair by age 12 and are six times more susceptible to any type of cancer. They could not be exposed to sunlight without serious injury. These deficiencies caused by the disease, of course, described what was happening with our son, Jose.

The usual life expectancy of these children was 17 years of age.

That was the good news.

The bad news was that although the symptoms of our three children were all different, all three of them were carriers of the disease and **there was no cure.**

Miriam and I did not know what to say. We had held on to the hope of a cure through the medical advances of the United States but the news was paralyzing.

The doctor explained that the gene had not been detected and that the disease was so rare that of the then 250 million people in the United States, only 700 families were affected. In the rest of the world there was only one patient in Chile, 3 in

Argentina, 2 in China and we were the first Bolivians ever to be diagnosed with the disease.

They called it the orphaned disease because neither government nor private agencies assigned any resources to investigate it since so few people would benefit from it and so the expense could not be justified.

As consolation, the doctor told us that there were two places where they were researching this condition. One was in California and the other in New York.

We were overcome with a sense of abandonment. We felt death itself hungrily surrounding us again. From that moment on, Miriam and I had no idea what awaited us. We could only wait for a miracle in which God could be glorified by healing our children.

The brothers and sisters at the church would help us as much as they could. The family with whom we stayed lovingly gave us food and shelter.

Some churches knowing that I was a well known pastor in Bolivia, would invite me and happily I would share the Word. At the end of the message, the pastors would come with an envelope with an offering for us. My ministerial dignity was offended because in my country we did not have the custom of receiving offerings for preaching the gospel. I felt that as a minister of God, He was my provision so much so that every time they gave us an envelope, I was surprised, but I would nonetheless accept it and give it to Miriam without opening it.

That went on for several weeks, until we made contact with Juan Carlos, pastor Salcedo's brother, whose wife was a nurse. She was yet another angel that God provided for us. She decided to take on my children's case and find help for them. She managed to make contact with medical scientists who were involved in researching the disease and they agreed to meet with us. They then found us a place to live with a Christian family who had two children.

We said good-bye to the brothers and sisters in Virginia and travelled to New York. In the interim, Lourdes Ursic succumbed to her illness and a few weeks later went to be with the Lord. We are sure that we will see her again when the Lord returns.

Carlos and Miriam in New York

In New York, Juan Carlos and Linda were very kind. Sarita and I stayed with them while Miriam accompanied Jose and Daniela to the hospital. They stayed there for 25 days. Their treatment did not cost a cent thanks to Linda's intervention.

"Though I walk in the midst of trouble, you preserve my life; you

stretch out your hand against the wrath of my enemies, and your right hand delivers me.“

Psalms 138:7

Our three children ended up getting very sick. Jose and Daniela had infections that the doctors were treating and Sarita was losing weight due to a minor infection. The doctors helped us to stabilize them and to take charge of the frequent conditions that arose from the Ataxia, especially the incontrollable coughing spells that plagued Jose. They gave us good medicines, a nebulizer for administering "albuterol", a medication that calmed him and we had many other resources available for every episode.

During the following 6 months Jose became remarkably better. So much so that he became mobile again and was gaining weight. Our hearts were joyful. Obviously, the doctors warned us that this was temporary since the disease was degenerative.

At this point, the pain in Miriam's soul began to show in her body and she began to manifest the effects of so many years of tension. Suddenly she could no longer sleep due to pain she felt throughout her body. She got to the point where she could no longer walk or do things for herself.

In the meantime, the people of the church in Virginia, in the Washington DC metropolitan area, had asked me to minister to them because they could not find a church like the one we had in Bolivia. So I travelled each week from New York to visit them and minister the Word to them.

Our battleground had been well defined. We knew what

it was that we were fighting. We had only two options left: a miracle or manage each day we had left with our children so that they could have the best life possible. Until now we had centered our lives on serving God and the church. Now the priority, after God, was our children, then the church and finally us.

Facing this reality was extremely difficult for Miriam and me. She was now showing physical signs of the pressure within and I started to crumble on seeing that my family could not lead a normal life.

"In all circumstances take up the shield of faith, with which you can extinguish all the flaming darts of the evil one."

Ephesians 6:16

For those who recognize the existence of a supernatural world, we know of demonic activity and how they can attack us with negative thoughts. One day, upon returning from meeting with the researchers in Linda's van, the atmosphere was filled with a powerful tension. Everyone was silent. Linda had had a very difficult day and in addition to her obligations, she had to carry the load of helping us. Suddenly these thoughts flooded my mind: *"My wife and I carry death inside of us. Maybe we should never have married each other? It is not right that my children should have to suffer for something that is not their fault. Why doesn't God do a miracle? This life doesn't make any sense. There is no way out of this tunnel. What I am living is no life at all, and it seems that God has forgotten about us. My children are suffering without hope of recovery. I think it would be better if they were in the presence of the Lord".*

We made our way down the highway and I noticed that

in this particular area there were many bridges and high places as the words in my mind kept tormenting me: *"I'm going to rent a car and place my children in it and drive so fast over one of those bridges that we will careen over the edge and die quickly. I won't take Miriam with us because she would have to decide for herself. I know that I will go to hell, but at least my children will be with the Lord. I can't stand this anymore."*

Suddenly the Holy Spirit spoke to me saying:

"Where is the pastor that preached to the multitudes saying: 'What can separate us from the love of Christ? Not death...not life...not...'"

'What are the thousands of people that you have guided in the ways of God going to say? How many of them will lose faith because of your actions?'

'Where is that confession in which you said: "In Christ we are more than conquerors?'"

"Where is that man who gave up everything and gave his life to God?"

I was bombarded by the thoughts and the questions of the Holy Spirit. He spoke to me very sternly that night. He didn't give me a pat on the back, but instead He confronted me with the very same messages that I had preached to others.

I poured myself out and spoke to Him knowing full well what was in me: *"Alright, alright, I won't do it. I won't kill myself...but don't torture me like this!"* I asked God for forgiveness and I asked Him for His help. I could not carry this load by myself.

CHAPTER 15

UNEXPECTED BLESSINGS

"the LORD make his face to shine upon you and be gracious to you;"

Numbers 6:25

Thanksgiving Day was over in 1994 and the winter and Christmas were fast approaching. Juan Carlos had found us a house to rent and share with a colleague of his from China.

Where were we going to get the money to pay for the rent? I couldn't work because I only had a tourist visa. The brothers from the church in Bolivia were no longer sending us a salary. Then we remembered the envelopes that had been given us when I preached in Virginia. We opened them and "Oh!" "Surprise!" There was enough money to pay for the rent, buy groceries and cover other household expenses for a period of 4 months. God had provided for us in advance by the generosity of the brethren. The offense that I felt on receiving the offering envelopes was turned into gratitude.

Juan Carlos had some furniture in storage so when we moved to the new house; we had all the basic pieces that we needed which was sufficient for us.

Every weekend we rented a car and traveled to Virginia to minister to the brethren there. This was the beginning of what is today our church, Ekklesia USA.

As the winter approached in 1994 and seeing our limited resources, we agreed not to do anything special for Christmas. I asked myself, "How many more Christmases would my children see?"

Miriam and the children, winter in New York

THE SALVATION ARMY

Our minds were completely focused on keeping our children away from any possible sources of infection in order to keep them healthy and as time passed, Linda had sprung into action once more. She could not conceive of our children not having a Christmas party so she began to look for organizations, churches or institutions who might be willing to give some gifts to this Bolivian family far away from home who was battling against an incurable disease. Whoever heard this description got a very bleak picture. Nonetheless Linda's efforts got no results. On the last try and just a few weeks before Christmas she called a church associated with the Salvation Army in the area. After explaining the situation, the person on the other end of the line gave a jubilant shout and began to praise God in a loud voice. Linda thought that the lady had misunderstood and that she may have thought that Linda was going to donate gifts to them.

Once the secretary calmed down, she explained that the pastor of the church had a crazy idea that year. Every year they would select a neighborhood in which to give out toys for Christmas. However, this particular year the pastor decided to do something different. They would look for a family in need and they would make them a Christmas party. After several weeks nobody in the congregation had come up with a family in need. It got so that the members were discouraged that this year they might not be able to fulfill the pastor's wishes, but Linda's call had changed all that.

On the appointed day, our children received all kinds of gifts, toys and winter clothes. In addition they gave us $500.00 that would help cover the household costs. We had a marvelous Christmas and we felt the embrace and the warmth of God's love through these generous people.

Christmas, 1994. New York

"My soul My soul clings to you; your right hand upholds me"

Psalms 63:8

In the meantime, the battle with our faith continued. The scientists from New York had managed to stabilize our children so that their lives became more bearable.

During one of the trips to Virginia, while I drove, I thought:

"I really don't understand this. What do I have to do? Lord, this burden is too great for me. I cannot carry it any further! It seems that you are not going to heal my children. If I accept the reality of their condition, will you help me to carry this load?"

God spoke to Miriam through a Psalm that profoundly ministered to us and that immediately made me feel strong and gave me peace and encouraged me greatly.

From that point forward we began to manage everything differently with a new perspective knowing that our children could die at any moment. Our objective was different now. We were no longer looking to be ministers used by God like before. Now we just wanted to be the best possible parents to these exceptional children that God had given us for a time. With that in mind, we took stock of our situation. We knew that medical services in our country were very limited and that our children could not receive the same care as they did in the United States. We spoke with the pastors who served with us in Bolivia and we told them of our intention of staying in the U.S. They responded saying that we had to return as soon as possible. The weight of such a large congregation was too great for them. It is not easy to pastor 12,000 people. The pastors decided to meet us in New York. We invited a pastor friend, J.C. Hedgecock, to sit in as an impartial observer and help us with this decision. After extensive conversations we concluded what the Lord wanted us to do was to return to Bolivia.

CHAPTER 16

"...AND BRING THEM AGAIN

...to the land that you gave to them and to their fathers."

2 Chronicles 6:25b

We had airline tickets that were only good for six months. We had stayed too long so that they were no longer valid.

After saying goodbye to Juan Carlos and Linda, we returned to Virginia where we stayed with a sister, Ana Luisa Cornejo, who lovingly received us. We also said goodbye to the small group of followers with whom we had started our church in Virginia, but who continued to meet weekly.

We arrived at the Miami airport with the expired tickets. Reading from the airline computer monitors the agents told us that we would have to buy new tickets for $3000.00. They motioned me to go speak with a supervisor to see if it was possible to just pay a penalty and renew the same tickets. Miriam and the children were seated with the bags asking Jesus to grant us a miracle. I was in line watching those who were attending the passengers in line. One of them was a lady of Asian descent who was in a really bad mood and who was denying every request put before her. Until my turn came, I intensified my prayer asking God not to allow her to be the one who would serve me and there she was in front of me.

She adjusted her attitude and asked me to state my case. I explained to her that our stay had been prolonged due to medical reasons. She asked how my children were doing and I told her they were better. She then asked for written proof of my story. I ran to get the letter from the hospital that was in Miriam's suitcase. The lady read the letter and was touched. She asked me what date I wanted to depart and I said, *"In three days"*. Her demeanor changed, she smiled at me and said, *"Fine, I am approving your tickets. You do not have to purchase new ones."* Then she smiled at me once more.

Hallelujah! We had just experienced a $3,000.00 miracle! It's really interesting how in the beginning some of our flesh and blood angels looked hostile to our needs, but God would grant us grace with them and they always ended up smiling and a miracle would happen.

We rented a car and traveled to Orlando to visit a couple who were friends of ours, Rick and Bette Strombeck, missionaries whom we greatly loved. We really wanted to take our kids to Disneyland. Rick and Bette gave us a car and we spent the whole day with the kids at Disneyland. It was a marvelous day!

Before returning to Bolivia. Florida, USA-1995

Within 3 days we were on our way back to Bolivia. On the flight, the Lord spoke clearly to me and said, *"I am the only One who is sending you back."* This word was very important as it would eventually play a vital role in what was to come.

The pulmonary specialist in New York had told us that due to the condition of our son's lungs he would live two more years at most. Then he said, *"How I wish I could do more for you!"* As he saw us depart he had a sad look on his face. We were like the Word says, as "sheep to the slaughter", but we were sure that it was God who was sending us back and we were to do the things that He had prepared for us beforehand.

Jose, Sarita and Daniela with the pediatric pulmonary specialist

I returned to my post as pastor of the church, we returned to our apartment and we were attended by the same doctors we had before we left. We informed them of the diagnosis that we had received in the United States and the precautions and care that had to be taken with our children. It was strange that the parents of the patients had to teach the doctors about an illness they were hearing about for the first time. That was the difference between the healthcare of one country over another. This was our reality and God was with us.

"Every charge must be established by the evidence of two or three witnesses"

2 Corinthians 13:1b

It was now December of 1995, the year in which two bullets took the life of our pastor, Julio Cesar Ruibal. He was murdered at the door of a church on his way to a pastor's meeting in Cali, Colombia.

Meanwhile in our church in La Paz, Bolivia, we were three pastors each with the same level of authority and decision making responsibilities. We were a team that the Lord had used to manage the tremendous blessings that we were experiencing. We decided on a leadership approach as a reaction to the one we had received from our founding pastor whose approach was more authoritarian. Our relationship was based on total dependence on God, the transparency of our actions, obedience to Biblical principles and seeking the will of God in unanimity. Along with the pastors of MFI (Ministers Fellowship International), who were our spiritual covering, we decided to modify this. From this point on we would have one pastor and two co-pastors. Pastor Alberto Salcedo was elected Senior Pastor.

As a family, we once again enjoyed a relatively peaceful life even though we had turned our tiny apartment into a small clinic with restricted access keeping it as disinfected and isolated as possible. When someone visited we made sure that they were not sick.

Miriam spent most of her time at home and only went out once in a while to get some rest or to restore her energy. I continued to travel and work on the vision as set out by the new leadership.

One day I asked God, *"Lord, this is not a complaint, or a disagreement with the decisions that have been made, be things as they are. I just have one question, 'Is there some special rea-*

son why You did not choose me as the Senior Pastor?'"

That question produced a response from heaven that I did not expect. *"Your time at Ekklesia Bolivia is over. You have finished the work that I sent you to do. I want you to prepare to hand everything over to the Pastor and get ready because I have a new mission for you."*

Pastor Salcedo did not believe me, nonetheless, the plan was already underway and God's plan was once again in motion.

While Ekklesia Bolivia faced new challenges being led by the new leadership, Miriam was carrying the load of the most difficult times in the health of the children. Along with handling the oxygen that Jose required, she had to organize the minutia of administering the antibiotics, control the fevers, go many nights without sleep and care for any injuries because the slightest infection could take their life before the time the doctors had indicated.

There are times in which the Lord does not take away our burden, but gives us strength to continue while making us better understand our mission. That's exactly what happened with Miriam.

Those missionary friends that we visited in Orlando, Florida, the Strombecks, had a missionary school in our home town. They had invested a great deal towards its development. They travelled to Bolivia once or twice a year to supervise it for a period of 10 years during which we developed a friendship of great blessing.

Every time they arrived, Bette Strombeck would take an afternoon to invite Miriam to share with her. Miriam was under a great burden and during these times, she took advantage of the opportunity to open her heart. That was often enough to make her feel better. She expected some type of consolation or maybe a prayer of support. What she got came directly from heaven and gave her a new mission, *"Miriam, you know that death is something natural that we all experience. God only knows when each of us will die. Now your children will also go to be with the Lord like all of us. It's just that God has given them a life that is very short. Like all parents you want your children to go to the presence of God when it is their time and you have the job of preparing them for that moment. You cannot miss this opportunity. You must prepare them to arrive in the presence of the Lord as soon as possible."*

After hearing those words, Miriam felt a powerful conviction of the Holy Spirit, understanding that the Lord was giving her the mission of preparing our children for their eternal home. She had little time to do this, but she faced the situation with renewed motivation, with a new mission and a new strength that came as the fruit from the lips of God through Bette. From that point on she taught our children about our heavenly home, about the Wedding Feast of the Shepherd and how we have white garments and about the Second Coming of Jesus. She did such a great job that my daughters longed for Jesus to come soon. They chose the clothes they would wear to the Wedding Feast and they prayed with the certainty that we could be there together as a family. Although they were very small, they were sure that they were saved and that Jesus waited for them in the house He was preparing for us.

Jose Esteban, 12 years old

We knew that at any moment Jose Esteban would go to be with the Lord. We waited for something supernatural, that miracle that would return him to health, but we also prepared for his departure. We did everything we could for him, but little by little his body was deteriorating. Time passed and by 1996 Jose was wheel chair bound. He was oxygen dependent 24 hours a day each day requiring more and more. Since he could not move on his own, he required physical therapy twice a day. He could no longer study due to his physical condition. During his last year he required constant attention to meet his needs. Every day Miriam carried a wide leather strap which she used to lift him up from his bed each morning and transfer him to his wheelchair and vice versa. He had to be helped to change positions constantly otherwise he would become very uncomfortable. So we adjusted him every hour day and night. Since Miriam was exhausted, we had to take turns during the night so she could rest and recuperate her strength a bit.

Jose was now 12 years old and even though his lung function was diminishing little by little, he never complained. He was a sweet and brave child.

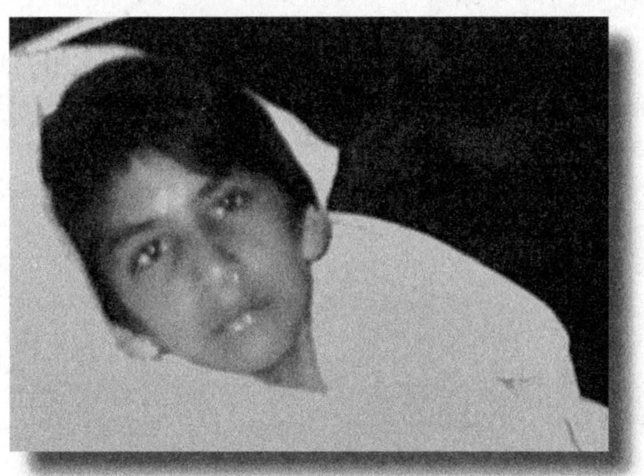

Jose Esteban, two days before he died

On the night of November 1st, we talked about what would happen. I told him that he would encounter the Lord, that he should not be afraid because he would be just fine. I didn't want him to see death as it is, but rather as a special moment that all of us have in order to reach the presence of God.

The morning of November 2nd, upon awakening, I asked him if he was hungry and he said, "Yes". Miriam prepared a papaya puree that he ate with difficulty. He loved to lie on his tummy on our bed and watch television. By nightfall we were in our bedroom. Jose had fallen asleep watching his favorite programs. I noticed that his respiration was weak. The girls were already asleep as it was about 11 p.m. Jose was in his last moments. A few minutes later his spirit passed on into the hands of the Lord. He died peacefully, without pain, without suffering and without saying a word. Jose died like a child of peace.

We notified our parents. We bathe his little body and dressed him in his favorite outfit which we had bought in Colombia and that he really liked and put his favorite tennis shoes on his feet. We left his little body on our bed as we slept by his side.

The next morning we notified everyone else. A wake was organized at the church where thousands of people came to be with us. Hundreds of them passed before us to embrace us, give us a word of encouragement and to cry with us. Many of the pastors in the city came to be with us and to support us. The words of one of them are engraved in my memory. He said, *"A servant is only allowed to look back quickly, wipe his tears and take up his plow and continue"*.

That was exactly what happened. The next day a long caravan formed. The children from Jose's class, dressed in their uniforms formed a pathway in the "Cementerio Jardin", where we finally laid our first born to rest and the son that my wife had always longed for. Miriam had such a great peace and she did not cry. On the one hand I was watching the lives of my children ebb away, but I was also witnessing the lives of thousands ignit-

During the funeral procession I experienced emotional ups and downs that were almost uncontrollable. There were moments in which I praised the Lord with all my strength joining my voice with the brethren. Then I would receive the words of consolation that they gave me, but when someone gave me a text from the Bible to encourage me it went straight into my spirit. I became aware of the power that the Word of God has to bring comfort in moments like these, making it much stronger than the most inspiring words from men.

"...because you have seen my affliction; you have known the distress of my soul,"

Psalms 31:7

Just looking at Miriam's peaceful face was something else. Pastor Salcedo's wife told Miriam that she had that peace because she had stayed with our son despite her strong calling to the ministry. She had finished her mission with Jose. Now our son was enjoying the presence of God.

It was true. Miriam had done a good job and the Spirit of God was not only comforting her but also giving her that peace that transcends all understanding.

The death of Jose was not a surprise to us, although I have to say that we held on to the hope of a miracle until the last moment. We had hope, we prayed, we had faith in Almighty God and we believed that He would be glorified in our two daughters that remained. We only needed for God to give the Word and the miracle would take place. Our lives were focused on that hope and in the ministry of the church with 12,000 witnesses seated in the first row!

What had escaped our notice were the thousands of brothers and sisters who found motivation and encouragement by the way that we were living and the way that God was strengthening us. Many times when they had a problem, they would think about us and say, *"If the pastor and his wife can keep going in the midst of so many challenges, how can I not go forward when my problems cannot begin to compare with theirs."*

CHAPTER 17

GRADUATION IN BOLIVIA

During this time the church was undergoing a series of fundraising campaigns to cover the enormous cost of maintaining the television network in a country like Bolivia and as a result many church members made pledges. They gave jewelry, cars and a variety of personal possessions which were lovingly placed as an offering.

In some cases, instead of presenting an offering to the church, God directed some of the people to give a special offering to the pastors. One day a well known brother from church came to my house. He was a businessman. After greeting me, he gave me a ring, one that he always wore, saying, *"God has spoken to my heart and he has motivated me to give you my ring."*

The truth is that I couldn't understand the offering because I have never been one to enjoy wearing jewelry especially something so ostentatious. He was so motivated that I did not refuse his offering.

Later while I was praying, I asked the Lord if he wanted to say something to me with this offering or if it was simply an act of love from this brother. God responded in an unexpected and surprising way. He said, *"This ring is for your graduation. You have finished your work here and I am giving you this ring as a gift because you have concluded the mission that I gave you here"*.

I felt great joy in my heart to hear God say to me that I

had finished my work in the same place where I had accepted the Gospel. This marked a great milestone in my life.

I had dedicated 22 years to Ekklesia Bolivia. I saw the birth of the church with my own eyes. I saw it pass through different stages. I took it by the hand through crisis and great moments of glory. I began to feel the enormous satisfaction of a father seeing his children reach their goals in life. That's how I felt in relation to my church.

The time had come to let her stand on her own and that made me feel very happy and satisfied in a way that only those who are truly spiritual parents can feel. I understood Paul's love for the churches he planted and built being their spiritual covering and their apostle.

In the natural realm my eldest son went on to be with the Lord. In the spiritual sense my eldest daughter, Ekklesia Bolivia, went forth into the hands of whoever would be its pastors in the future.

SARA CONSUELO

Two weeks later from the day that Jose went to be with the Lord, we were now only Sara, Daniela, Miriam and I. The church was in full transition adapting to the new leadership structure that we had implemented, when one day we received a call from one of our angels. Linda had continued with the commitment she had made to herself to help my children. It seemed that the defective gene that was causing our children's illness had been identified in Israel. This produced a series of changes in the management and support available to families who had this genetic condition. Many organizations were now committing resources to investigate the illness like the world famous Johns Hopkins Hospital in Baltimore, MD. They had opened a clinic to help patients afflicted with this illness.

Johns Hopkins Hospital, Baltimore, Maryland

The call from Linda, nevertheless, was also troubling. She had sent recent photographs of Sara to Johns Hopkins, showing the inflammation on her skin and some sores that had appeared on her face and body. Our daughter had been sleeping a lot more than normal. She was always swollen and she had a strange allergy. It was obvious that something was up. Linda said the doctors had seen the pictures of Sarita and were asking for us to bring her to the hospital as quickly as possible.

We were not done grieving for Jose and again we found ourselves at the threshold of a radical change in our lives. There was no time to waste. Just like before, the Lord supernaturally provided the resources so we could travel. At first we thought that I would just go with Sara, but Miriam did not like the idea. On the 6th of December of 1996 we stepped on American soil once again leaving behind two children whom we had buried, a church in the throes of a revival and a family that could not comprehend what was happening in our lives.

"In distress you called, and I delivered you; I answered you in the secret place of thunder; I tested you at the waters of Meribah."

Psalms 81:7

MALIGNANT LYMPHOMA

This time we arrived in the state of Maryland. The Bejarano family allowed us to stay with them. They had been part of the church in Bolivia and had emigrated two years ahead of us. They were a family of 6 living in one apartment; parents, three children and a nephew that lived with them. We were 4 more, but they received us with great love. They embraced us and despite the crowding, they saw no problem with the inconvenience and the limits we were placing on their space. Through them we felt the love of Christ and the respect they had for us as pastors.

The hospital had notified me that the treatment would cost $15,000.00, but that I could give $6,000.00 down and the rest could be paid in installments. The Lord miraculously provided the money and we arrived to begin our new odyssey. We thought we would be in the U.S. a maximum of 2 months but just the diagnostic process alone took that long.

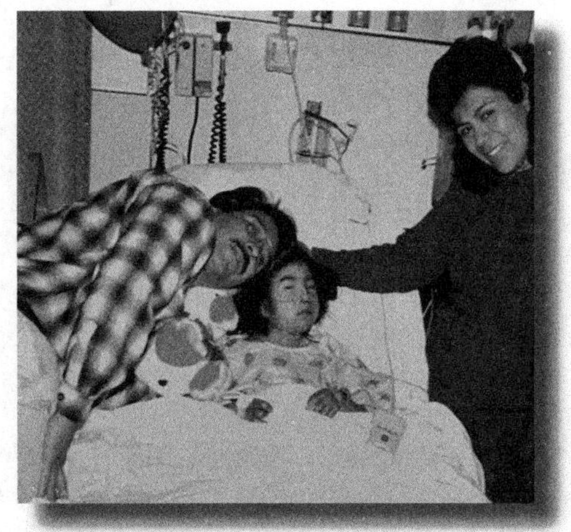

Carlos, Miriam and Sarita in Intensive Care

JOHNS HOPKINS HOSPITAL

After many tests, they concluded that the problem was not with Sara's skin, so they changed their protocol which caused the cost to skyrocket.

We decided that due to my proficiency in English, I would stay with Sarita in the hospital and communicate with the doctors. As always Sara was very happy to have her "papi" by her side. It was the first time that I would spend so much time with her. So my heart began to really open up to Sara's love.

The money that we had for the treatment of her skin was now gone. The doctors decided to conduct several diagnostic examinations including a bone marrow biopsy.

Medical care in the United States is very different than what we experienced in our country. Something that always surprised me was how the doctors and nurses took special care to ensure that the children were not traumatized, feel insecure or have any unnecessary pain above and beyond their current condition. Because of this I was able to be present by Sara's side through all her procedures and make her feel secure and confident since she had her daddy with her. This was very good for Sara.

The weight of her suffering touched me deeply especially when she went through her spinal tap. She was sedated but awake. She would not be able to remember this later. I, on the other hand, was fully conscious holding her hand by her side. I could see, feel and suffer the pain of my little Sara. In more than one instance I was at the point of telling the doctors to stop the treatment because my child would squeeze my hand with all her might. She would cry with deep groanings so intensely that I would fall apart inside wanting to say, "No more! Leave her alone! I don't want her to suffer anymore!" Nonetheless I would hold on because I knew that this was the only way that they would find out what was happening to our child. One more time I had to suffer the physical pain of the moment so that a ray of hope would appear, so that we could gain some advantage in Sarita's condition.

Our daughter's condition was so unusual that they went on to be research subjects for the hospital. Specialists and genetic engineers took it upon themselves to look for the cause of the problems they had. Our own blood was analyzed so many times. According to the scientists there was a 25% chance that the children of the genetic carriers would be sick with the disease, but in our case it was 100%. One day on our way to the consultation room, I asked two of the geneticists, "*Why?*". They responded, "*Extremely bad luck!*" Immediately a battle broke out inside me, but the Holy Spirit of God said to me, *"Each one of your children was planned and sent by Me with a purpose in this world."* Instantly the peace of the Lord filled me and gave me rest.

After much medical testing, some of them very painful, the doctors diagnosed what was happening with my daughter. It was a malignant lymphoma in her spinal fluid. It caused her body to produce excessive amounts of blood plasma and in her case gave her chronic problems with her skin and other symptoms.

This particular type of cancer had never before been seen in a child. It was a lymphoma that only attacked men and then only those over 60 years of age. No one had ever treated a child for this condition.

The best the doctors said they could do was to adjust the required 6 adult doses of medication to her small size and her age. They also told us that she would receive another treatment in addition. They would connect Sara to a machine that would separate her blood plasma from her red blood cells and replace them with healthy plasma. To accomplish this they placed a catheter in one of her coronary arteries to eliminate the need of injecting her every time that she needed the treatment. That catheter, called a Hickman catheter, would make her treatment easier and help to make her more comfortable, but it would be necessary to keep it sterile and every three days it had to be disinfected, cleaned and covered again leaving only the external contacts exposed. That needed to be done by a nurse, but since we had no insurance, the doctors had to train me to do it.

I would cover my nose and mouth with a sterile mask,

wash my hands carefully and put on sterile gloves. I would open a surgical kit and start the process which took 30 minutes. Every 3 days I would do this with great care and love while our little Sara felt confident since it was her dad who was caring for her.

I trembled and perspired each time I had to do it because I knew that the slightest distraction could cause an infection to enter her blood stream directly and risk her life. It was a procedure that the family watched from a distance, but it had become so common that one time the nurses started the process and Sara stopped them. When they asked her why, she said, *"I want my daddy to do it"*. The nurses said, *"Of course! We will let daddy do it."*

That day I sweated three times more than usual because I had to do it in front of the nurses. When it was over they congratulated me and told me that I could come to work at the hospital as an nurse assistant. I'm sure they were joking.

I must have done a good job because Little Sara never got an infection. Just when I thought this would be the extent of my participation in medical procedures for my daughter, the doctors told me that I would have to give her daily injections. They had to be given in her little arm or her leg. After they instructed me on how to administer them, I could only respond by saying, *"But I've never given an injection to anyone before!"* One of the nurses responded as though it was the most common occurrence, *"I'll teach you."* The next thing I knew, she's explaining how to do this using an orange. I said, *"I understand, but I think it will be much different doing this to a human being."* She answered quickly, *"OK. Try it on me!"* and she rolled up her sleeve and handed me the syringe. My hands had never trembled so much in my life. I broke out in a cold sweat. I had to do it! My daughter's health depended on it.

God bless those nurses. More than once they went out of their way. Still today I am greatly moved by their sensitivity towards us.

I became the head nurse for my daughter. I became an expert in treatments and injections and Sara was always secure with daddy by her side. My heart became one with little Sara and I came to love her in a very profound way. Any thought of keeping a distance from her completely vanished. Now I was fighting for her with everything that I had at my disposal. Once again I had faith, motivation and all of my being was in battle mode hoping that something good would come from all of this.

In order to treat the malignant lymphoma in her spine, the doctors said that she required six sessions of chemotherapy. The first doses produced a marvelous result and her skin cleared up completely. Sara was alert and active. Happy as I was, when we were home, I would take my guitar and she would come running to my side from wherever she was to listen and lay her head on my shoulder. Any time we praised and worshiped our Heavenly Father, whether at home or at church, she always rejoiced.

One month later the time had arrived for the second dose. It also produced good results, but she became a little weak to the point that we had to limit her contact with others so she couldn't contract anything. This, of course, would have been fatal for her.

After some tests, the oncologist came looking for us to give us the results and he told us that there was no trace of the lymphoma.

It had completely disappeared!

We felt that God was performing a miracle and there was great joy in our hearts. We immediately sent word to the brothers in Bolivia. We were all so completely overjoyed!

CHAPTER 18

THE DRESS, HOLY COMMUNION AND THE ENCOUNTER WITH GOD

It was now winter of 1997. A small group of believers that met with us was now our only ministerial activity. About 20 people met with us on Saturday nights. The presence of God was exactly the same as when 3000 people met in each of the 4 services at the "Casa de la Casa" (House of the House) in our native Bolivia. His presence didn't depend on the number of people present, but on the sincerity of their worship.

I had promised little Sara that if she would agree to another treatment that she didn't want to undergo, I would let her go to town with her mother and let her buy whatever she wanted. She agreed to this "bribery" and submitted herself for examination.

Once downtown she picked out a beautiful blue floral dress along with a hat and matching white gloves. She tried it on at home and I thought, *"When we return to Bolivia, she could show off that beautiful dress and we will present her healed before the entire congregation."* She looked so beautiful!

That particular Saturday it was quite cold. Miriam and I had decided that I would go to the church service alone. We had prepared to serve the Lord's Table which was quite an event for us, but I didn't want to take the girls because Daniela had a fever and it was very complicated for little Sara as well due to her chemotherapy. Her immune system was so weak that we had to protect her respiratory system with a mask and filter, watch her carefully and bundle her up since the most minor of infections could have fatal consequences.

When Sara heard that she could not go, she began to cry because she said she wanted to participate in the Lord's Supper. Miriam and I thought that she was expecting food at the service and possibly even dessert. To discourage her, we explained that there would only be a small morsel of bread and some wine and that there would definitely not be any other food. She insisted surprisingly, *"I know. I want to go."*

We decided that Miriam would stay home with Daniela and I would go with Sara. The service was very beautiful. That day we were about 15 people. After blessing the bread, one of the sisters approached me to say that Sara also wanted to take communion. I asked my daughter if that is what she wanted to do warning her that the wine didn't taste very good. Solemnly she responded, "*Papi, I want to participate*. I acquiesced. ("*... for to such belongs the kingdom of heaven.*" *Matthew 19:14b*)

When I blessed the wine, I looked at Sara. There was such a special glow upon her face! She took the elements with such a consecrated expression and with such solemnity that anyone could plainly see what it meant to her. I knew that Sara had a supernatural encounter with her Lord. It was one of those celestial moments when one touches eternity and it was happening to our daughter. It was something so special that it was impossible to ignore. It was the moment of preparation for what she would face just a few days later. It was about something so solemn like when the woman washed the feet of Jesus, she dried His feet with her hair and the Lord said to His disciples, "*...Why do you trouble the woman? For she has done a beautiful thing to me... In pouring this ointment on my body, she has done it to prepare me for* *burial." (Matthew 25:10b,12)* They had not understood that it was about something prophetic.

Little Sara was renewing her covenant with Jesus in preparation for meeting Him face to face in just a few more weeks.

She had asked me if she could wear the new dress that I had bought her, but I discouraged her from wearing it. This is one of the few things that I still feel badly about, because Sara only got to wear it the day of her burial. I had prevented her from wearing it the day that she renewed her covenant with Jesus.

IT IS FINISHED

When our beloved savior was on the cross, taking on our sins to justify us, He said, ***"It is finished."*** Then He gave up His Spirit. There was no need for Jesus to spend one more minute on the earth. His work was done. I understood this truth much better when I understood that Sara's mission was over and that there was no need for her to stay one minute longer on the earth. My heart had been healed of what I was not even aware of; the pain of thinking that loving my daughters would somehow cause their deaths.

Now I was completely healed. I deeply and intensely loved my daughter Sara. I admired the courage she showed through all the medical procedures. Despite all her limitations she was happy because she had her daddy whom she loved so much, all to herself all that time.

The love that Sara gave me was so huge that once when she found out I was going on a trip she asked her mother's permission to help pack my bag. Miriam told me that despite the fact that her fingers were slightly curved from her illness and that her dexterity was therefore limited, she took a long time to fold and button my shirt, but she did this with all the love that God had given her. When I got to the hotel and saw my shirt and remembered how hard it had been for her to button it, I put it on with tears in my eyes. I used it to preach to the multitude and I know that during those moments, God was looking down on me.

With all these things Little Sara kept winning over my heart until I loved her in a way that I cannot describe. She touched my deepest sentiments and she became one of the most precious gifts in my life and her suffering became my suffering.

Sara was sent to love and to give without expecting anything in return. She was the instrument in the hands of God to confirm the healing of my heart and she showed me how to love again. The many months that she was in the hospital were the times when I learned to love her the most and was the closest to her. Sara got better and so we decided that it was time to return to Bolivia with our children. We told the doctors and they said there was no problem, but since we were so close to the time for the third dose of chemotherapy, they asked if we would allow it to be administered so that the last three doses could be administered in Bolivia. We thought that was a good idea and so we did it.

In March of 1997 when Sara was 7 years old she received the third dose of chemotherapy. Patients who receive this suffer a drop in white blood cells requiring multiple blood transfusions to compensate for continuous hemorrhaging.

We had made several trips to the hospital for this purpose. We were on the interstate. Little Sara was at my side lying on the seat of the vehicle that had been lovingly lent to us by the cousin of the family with whom we stayed. We were listening to Christian music in English when Sara says to me, *"Look, Daddy."* A huge blood clot had come out of her mouth. I had to catch it in my hand while I drove. She had the look of fear in her eyes. Reaching in for strength where there was none, I said, *"It's ok, my little one. Don't worry. We are going to the hospital so they can help you. Everything will be alright."*

A cold chill ran through my body and a huge worry inundated me. While holding that huge blood clot in my hand, I prayed, *"My God...and now what is waiting for us?"*

Little Sara was at ease with the words I had spoken to her. Now it was I that was scared and worried. I sank into a great silence only to find an empty echo inside that yielded no answers. There was only silence and the presence of that fear that makes one feel powerless, defenseless and vulnerable.

The music CD continued playing. The car sped down route I-95 at an impressive speed in the direction of Baltimore and my heart automatically went into an emergency mode which was very familiar to me. Hunger disappeared, time ceased to exist, and sleep was ignored until exhaustion took over.

I had only one thought; to do the impossible for Sara to be well. That was it.

Sara was admitted to the hospital. She quickly received the blood transfusion that she needed, but they discovered something in her lungs that was causing a fever. It was possibly a virus perhaps pneumonia. She spent some days in a regular hospital room until she went into crisis and they had to move her to intensive care. She was sedated and then intubated so that the machines could breathe for her. There I fell into a deep and questioning sadness as I battled for the life of my daughter. I decided to start a fast for her healing. Eight days passed and I stayed at her side as the hours and the days crept by without any positive change. The nurse insisted that I rest. At times she would throw me out of the room saying, *"Get some rest. Go eat!"*

Nothing else was important to me. I found myself glued to the side of Sara's bed, my Little Sara, the one who had healed my heart. I was watching her life be extinguished like a candle.

Several days had passed and her condition did not change. I was depleting along with my daughter until a nurse told me that there was no need for me to be there. Someone would call me if there was any change.

On April 17th the telephone rang while I was home with Miriam and Daniela. It was the hospital. They needed me to come urgently. Something had happened.

When I arrived they were taking Sara to do brain function studies using tomography. She had suffered a crisis. When I asked questions of the technician who was taking her for the exam, he said, *"This will help us to make decisions."*

After the examination the doctors called me and told me, *"At first her lungs were not responding and we were unable to improve them. Then her liver began to have problems and we were able to manage it somewhat. Now her kidneys are not functioning well. Three major bodily functions not working well is something that we cannot manage. In addition, you need to know that she is more dead than alive at this point. She will not recover. It is time to make a decision. It is time to disconnect her."*

I went home to get Miriam so that we could be together for this very serious moment. The director of Intensive Care Unit approached us and made it a point to say to us, *"I have known bad parents who abandoned their children. I have known very good parents and average parents, but you are exceptional parents. Let me just say to you that I admire you."* By this time almost all the nurses, doctors and medical students knew us well. We had passed through the care of many of them and now we were at the most difficult part of the process.

The room was filled with doctors and nurses and while they explained to us what was about to happen, I saw Miriam separate herself from the group and stand by Sara's bed close to her head and I overheard her say these words, *"Little Sara, today you are going to die. Today you are going to see our Lord. You are going to our home in heaven. I have a special request. When you see our Lord Jesus, I want you to ask Him to help your daddy handle your death. I am very concerned about him. I don't think he will be able to stand the pain of losing you, so please the first thing I want you to do when you get there is to ask Jesus to help your daddy. Ok, my love?"* I kept silent but I thought to myself, *"My wife has lost her mind!"* Everything was ready now. The nurses began to disconnect Sara from the machines.

They turned off the machines that kept her alive and they placed her in our arms to wait for her heart to stop beating.

When the moment came, Little Sara was lying in her mother's arms and I was by her side. They made us place her on the bed and they waited to give us time with her. Miriam got close to Sara's little head, she adjusted her in the way that only she could do and when we felt that there was nothing more that we could do, we walked out of intensive care and left.

CHAPTER 19

JOB

Miriam and I went down to the hospital cafeteria. We were face to face. Each of us lost in our own thoughts.

Miriam had gone through all this suffering by my side without complaining, without lamenting or questioning. She was the only one with whom I could share my pain. From deep within me I began to share my frustration. "*Why is God doing this to me? Why does He treat me like His enemy? All I have ever done is serve Him since my conversion! If He no longer has a heart for me, I will cease to exist. Why doesn't He just make me disappear once and for all? What does He want from me? I don't understand any of this!*" Without realizing it, I was repeating the words of Job in the middle of his crisis.

Later Miriam said she responded and tried to console me, but I didn't remember anything. I just remembered her being speechless. Maybe I just couldn't hear her. I just needed to express my grief and my confusion for the lack of results of all our prayers, fasting and all the other things that we had learned in all our years of ministry. Things that had worked and that had produced miracles for so many people to whom we had ministered, but for me they produced nothing.

We returned to the apartment and told the family whom we were staying with that our daughter had died. They cried as one would expect and they stood with us in our pain.

THE FUNERAL, THE VISION AND COMFORT

I became aware rather quickly that I could not become paralyzed by the pain. I was the decision maker. Regretfully, I realized that we had to bury our daughter and I had no idea how to do that. I did not know the system in this country and neither did I have any idea about the cost. This was something new I had to learn while burying my own daughter. I felt such an overwhelming sense of powerlessness. I didn't know what to do, where to go or whom to seek out. How do you bury a loved one in a foreign country where you do not know the laws or even the procedures to do this? What a dilemma! What pain! What do I do?

I remembered that the first family that had taken us in when we arrived in the U.S. had buried the wife's mother in Virginia. So perhaps they could give me some advice. I called them and they gave us the name of a Colombian woman who helped us immensely. She became another one of our angels. She came to our home to guide us through the process and she helped us find a funeral home that would take care of everything. When I asked how much it would cost, she said $5,000. I thought I would faint! There was no way that we had that kind of money! I was terrified that we would not be able to bury our daughter. I told her that we didn't have the money and she began to find solutions to our problem. She said, "*OK. We are going to cut out everything we can and see where we end up. Which church shall we use for the memorial service of your daughter?*" I had no idea. I wasn't familiar with any churches. We could only do something at the cemetery. "*That will save us $400. Who will be the pastor that will conduct the funeral?* I told her that I was a pastor and I would celebrate the funeral myself. She responded, "*Good. That will save us another $400*". We continued the conversation and finally we got to the minimum that the funeral would cost me: $3000. I didn't have it and she could not find a cheaper price.

Then I remembered that Juan Carlos, Linda's husband and brother of the pastor of the Bolivian church were we worked, had told me many times that someone had sent me an offering from Bolivia. He had procrastinated sending it to me for several months. I thought that this money could help us with the cost. So I contacted him by phone.

I told him that my daughter had died and I asked him if he could send me that offering now. He said he would send it the next day. When I asked him the amount, he said it was exactly $3000. God had provided for that moment and in His wisdom He allowed it to be sent when we needed it. His hand was with us in the midst of our suffering.

I called the Colombian lady and told her that we had the money and that it would arrive the next day. We made an appointment to visit the cemetery and select a place where we wanted to bury our little daughter.

We arrived at a place called The Garden of Remembrance in the city of Laurel, Maryland. We chose a lovely place next to a tree. The funeral director left us alone at the place where we were to bury little Sara. When he was gone, there we stood the three remaining members of the Penaloza family, Miriam, Daniela and me. We had been a family of 6 and now we were down to half of that. We meditated on that when suddenly I began to feel a joy in my heart that I could not understand. Then a great pride overtook me like something very special had just happened. The next thing I knew a vision came to me.

I must have been suspended in mid air because I was looking down on a scene. At some distance to my left I could see some wooden steps that went up like those on a pyramid and at the top there was a very bright light. I knew that God was there with His hands outstretched. At the base of the steps and on either side of a dirt road there were people standing like they were waiting for someone special to pass. At the beginning of the road was little Sara dressed in a white, somewhat transparent garment. On her little head were laurel and olive branches like those worn by ancient Olympic champions. She walked with a triumphant air about her while looking to one side and I, her father, found myself suspended in the air watching the events as they unfolded. I felt my heart filled with pride and satisfaction like when a parent watches his child receive a winning prize. That was exactly what I was feeling.

When the vision was over, I looked at Miriam and I told her the vision I had seen. She said that she hadn't seen anything, but that she felt the same pride and joy. We became aware that God had allowed us to see and feel in the spirit what was happening to our daughter. She was entering into the joy of her Lord and she was going up the steps to be with Him. She had already received her award. She had finished her work here on earth and now her crown of glory and the reward that God had prepared for her awaited her for a job well done. There I understood that Sara was sent to console me and she had done this in such a way that when she died, she left no pain behind. Immediately after the vision ended, all pain and sadness disappeared from my heart. Although here on earth I was going to bury the body of my daughter, God had already let me see what was happening in heaven and there things were very different. My daughter walked in her reward and she had no pain or sadness on her face. It was exactly the opposite. She was full of glory and filled with a sense of mission accomplished…or to put it in biblical terms…IT IS FINISHED, just as our beloved Lord had done on the cross.

Daniela, Miriam and I went out of the cemetery happy, praising God and singing. In the cemetery we touched eternity and God had healed our deep hurt and changed our sadness into joy. He had opened our eyes to see what was happening in heaven while He simultaneously consoled and healed our hearts.

Little Sara had accomplished her mission; the one her mother had given her, asking God to help me and He, in all His mercy, had responded to her request allowing me to see what was happening in heaven, something more real than the temporary death that we were experiencing. Our consolation came from life far beyond death. Our present reality was only temporary. Our true eternal reality was far beyond death.

"O death, where is your victory? O death, where is your sting?"

1 Corinthians 15:55

We understood that little Sara had finished her work on the earth, but that in heaven she was starting a new life. That comforted us because we know that she is only asleep, that her spirit and those of all my children are alive. We are certain that we will see them again when Christ returns or when we also die.

Two or three days later we celebrated her funeral. There were about 15 people in attendance. Among them was Dr. Finkelstein of Johns Hopkins University Hospital and one of the nurses.

In my message that day, the doctor told me that he heard

something he had never heard before. "*Many parents give their children healthy bodies, others give them athletic bodies and still others, as in our case, give them sickly bodies. But God gave our children a perfect spirit. Our children accomplished the purpose for which they were sent into this life in a very short time.*"

It has been 15 years since Sara died and we have never felt the pain of her departure. We always remember her with affection. We established "Casa Sarita" (Little Sara's House) in her memory, a ministry that takes in abandoned children in Bolivia. We care for these children, educate them under the loving care of their adoptive parents who treat them as their own.

Little Sara came, she loved and after she consoled my heart, she left making sure that her departure would not even leave any pain behind. She was complete consolation which is why I always say that she should have been named Sara Consuelo (Consolation).

To this day my wife and I live with that consolation and with the strength that was left to us when she entered into eternity. Glory be to our Lord Jesus Christ! Praise to His name!

Chapter 20

BEING ESTABLISHED WHERE HE PLACED US

Miriam, Carlos and Daniela

Daniela was the last child we had left and she was undergoing treatment. The hope of hearing good news regarding her healing was disappearing. Miriam and I decided it was time for us to return to Bolivia. While we were packing our bags, in the midst of my regular prayers, I heard the voice of the Lord say, ***"Do not return to your country. Stay here and establish a vision in this place. This is the new mission that I told you I had for you."***

This word meant great changes for us and my answer was, *"Lord, if this is from you, I need for you to confirm it with the other pastors with whom I work because you know that we work in unity. If I stay in this country it will require great changes for the leadership, for the church and for the ministry in Bolivia"*.

I wrote an e-mail to the pastor in Bolivia explaining what had happened and asking that he pray with his wife that we could receive a word from the Lord. A week later on a Tuesday on the day when the leadership routinely met, I received a call. It was the confirmation. God confirmed that my family and I should stay. Pastor Salcedo said that they had prayed and that they felt peace regarding this matter. He said they knew that it was God who was speaking to me about staying in the United States and starting a new Ekklesia.

I made a short trip to Bolivia to say goodbye to the church, make some legal arrangements and finally the congregation, the pastors and the multitude of those in attendance, prayed for me and my family in a final service. These were very emotional days during which I said goodbye to many individuals whom I led for many years.

Eight months had passed since we first began living with the Bejarano family who had been so patient with us. Since it was now decided that we would stay in the United States, we decided that I would begin to look for a place where we could live and Miriam would go to Bolivia with Daniela to get our belongings, sell whatever goods she could, empty out our apartment and speak to the pastors to see if they were willing to help us with the move. We were closing out 22 years of service to a vision. We were not able to bring the few things that we owned. We thought the church would support us. We were after all, co-founders of the church, the senior pastors and the ones who had taken the vision of the Lord to completion. We had earned the right to be supported by the church to which we had given our lives to.

"Who serves as a soldier at his own expense? Who plants a vineyard without eating any of its fruit? Or who tends a flock without getting some of the milk?"

1 Corinthians 9:7

Unfortunately, the pastors were influenced by people who were ambitious and who had bad intentions and within a short time they turned their backs on us. Miriam and I were left alone to begin a new stage in our ministry. We had lost our little daughter, Sara, and we also lost our spiritual daughter, Ekklesia Bolivia.

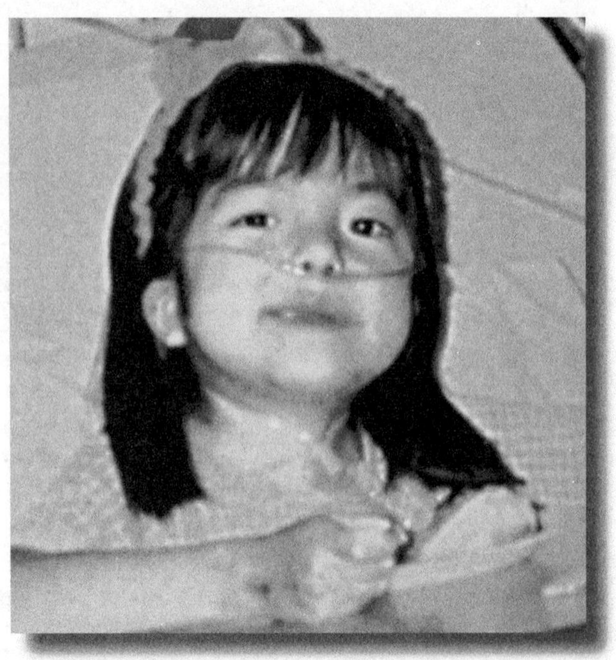

Daniela at 5 years old during one of her hospitalizations

DEPRESSION?

God had miraculously provided the money to buy a vehicle by way of a disciple whose family loved us very much. He was generous with us and we bought a van before Miriam travelled to Bolivia. Now we needed an apartment and for that we needed another miracle because to rent one in the United States you have to have a credit history. We didn't have one.

I visited many places that had vacancies, but when they asked me to fill out the application and saw that I had no credit history, everyone rejected me.

In the midst of all the hustle and bustle, I was overcome with one thought, *"I have so much peace inside that I don't un-*

derstand. I just lost my daughter, Sara, and I should feel at least a little sadness". The more I tried and searched inside me, the less I could find even a little sadness. It was something that my mind could not comprehend. It wasn't logical. It wasn't natural. It wasn't acceptable!

I decided to go to the city of Laurel in Maryland. I went to the cemetery and stood at the gravesite of my daughter so that I could feel the sadness that I felt I should have. To make the experience even more real, I took along the music CD that I used to play in John's pick-up truck as I took my daughter to the hospital and I listened to it for the 40 minute trip to get there. I remembered the time we heard a then famous Christian band while listening to "DC Talk" and traveling on Interstate 95 North toward Johns Hopkins. My daughter Sara had placed that huge blood clot in my hand. I recalled trying to calm my anguish, saying, *"It's ok, my little one. Don't worry."* That memory seemed perfect for helping me feel the natural sadness that I thought I should feel.

Once I arrived at the gravesite, oblivious to Miriam and Daniela's presence, with the music that flooded the area from my vehicle and standing before Sara's gravesite I expected that grief would overwhelm me.

I waited five minutes, then ten, and then fifteen and nothing happened. The peace of God had taken a hold of me beyond anything that I could comprehend. There was no room for sadness in my heart. Frustrated I turned off the music, started up the van and started the journey back home. A few minutes away from the cemetery I decided to take what I thought was a shortcut. It was a two lane road lined on both sides with lots of trees, weed and undergrowth. Suddenly, the engine on the van stopped. I was able to maneuver quickly to the side of the road to try to start the engine again. Nothing happened. I waited a while to try again, but again nothing happened. The van was new but it wasn't working. I was forced to call a tow truck, but they asked me to find a gas station or a more appropriate place to pick me up because the place where the car had stalled had no visible location markings. Finally, after several tries, I was able to reach a gas station where again the van stalled. I waited about an hour. It was getting dark by now. The tow truck arrived and was kind enough to take me to a car rental place because I had no other way of getting home.

Two hours later, tired, hungry and this time very depressed, I arrived at the apartment where we were staying. No one was home. I decided to pray and ask God why my new vehicle was now in need of repair. Now I was really depressed.

Suddenly, in the way that only God responds, I felt His presence and I heard His voice with an explanation that, as often happened, made my jaw drop, "*You wanted to get depressed and feel sad for the loss of your child, but let me tell you that the peace that you have comes from me and not from your own mind. I have placed it there and no one can change that. I have definitively healed you and it is a healing that links your spirit to My Spirit. That is why you do not understand it. You could not make this happen yourself. So don't ask why you don't understand that peace.*

You wanted to feel sad about something? Well, I have given you something to be sad about. You can feel sad about your car, but not about your daughter. You are definitely healed because this is something between your spirit and mine. Don't try to understand it because your mind cannot comprehend it.

Simply enjoy it".

Truly when God heals our wounds He does it completely. He does it perfectly. He is Jehovah Rapha, our healer. We are convinced that the Lord's healings are real so much so that when I had a chance to speak with apostle Dick Iverson, he said *"I have known others who have gone through difficult situations and you can see the marks of the experiences on their faces. However, when I see and hear you, your face doesn't reflect any mark or sign of your suffering".* Glory to God once more! He did His work completely!

PROVISION

Finally, after an exhaustive search, I found an apartment building with vacancies. When I entered the office a very nice lady attended me. When I entered the vacant apartment I was overcome with great peace and I had the conviction that this was the place where I would live with my wife and daughter.

This time I didn't wait to be asked for my credit history, I simply told her that I didn't have any. She wasn't the least bit concerned. *"Can you acquire a letter that says you have a monthly income?"* I told her I could and she said to me, *"That should suffice because we get many people here who work with international organizations and we don't have any trouble accepting them."* I got the letter. We finally had a place to call our own.

Miriam and Daniela returned from Bolivia and came directly to our new apartment. Our furniture consisted of a donated bed and the dinnerware of a relative who had passed away. We had no dining or living room furniture, but we had a roof over our heads, a vehicle to get us around and the word of God directing us to establish a vision in the metropolitan area of Washington, DC.

The next step would be to establish the church which up to now had been a group of people with whom we met each Saturday night in a church basement for $500 a month, a sum that we struggled to pay.

Ekklesia USA in the beginning, Virginia

One of the first things I did after announcing that we were staying in the U.S. was to tell the members of the church that we were changing our services to Sunday mornings. They said, *"It isn't possible to find a church that will rent to us on a Sunday morning, because the churches themselves use their buildings at that time."* I said we would look elsewhere. We considered a hotel. The Holiday Inn in Arlington, Virginia would charge us $480 a week. We launched in faith. We began Ekklesia USA the first week of September in 1997 with the help of 45 people and a first offering of $800. Since then God has always sustained us so that today Ekklesia USA is a well established church in the metropolitan Washington DC area with 850 members not only consisting of Latin Americans, but also American and people of other nationalities. Services are simultaneously translated into English and transmitted by radio, and also sent by internet to various parts of the world.

Ekklesia is our last child in terms of churches unless the Lord tells us otherwise. For me and Miriam, Ekklesia USA will be the last church that we will personally start. All the future churches that will be birthed from our ministry shall be the progeny of Ekklesia USA.

Ekklesia USA today

CHAPTER 21

THE INSURANCE MIRACLE

Daniela was the one who suffered most often from infections, but she was also the one who benefitted most from our stay in the United States. Thank God that for her we had already gotten health insurance. We had acquired it through another miracle like so many that we experienced as a witness to God's provision throughout our journey.

When Sara was in the hospital, as I mentioned earlier, all the money we had with us was gone in one week. When they told me that they needed more tests and that we should worry about the bill later, I had no other option. I agreed and we went on. The months passed and with each exam, for each X-ray, scan, tomography, biopsy, physical therapy and whatever else they did, I signed the authorizations and everything was being charged to an account in my name. After a while I became concerned because I knew the total was mounting and it had to have become an enormous sum. I knew we needed another miracle to cover the hospital bills.

In the middle of the treatments, the finance office informed me that my debt had risen to a staggering $230,000. In my entire life I had never had that much money pass through my hands, and now I owed that much for the medical services provided to my daughters. My first reaction was to work it off. All I had to offer them was me so I would pay them back with my work for the rest of my life.

One of the sisters in the congregation suggested that

I visit a social worker in the state of Maryland. I had already spoken to the social worker at Johns Hopkins Hospital and I was assured that there was nothing that could be done. I spoke to the new social worker anyway. I told her the story of my family. She was touched by what I told her. She asked me if one of my daughters was presently in the hospital. I said, *"Yes"*. Then she said, *"The state can cover an emergency with the visa that you have"* and she sent me to the office of social services.

There I saw many people who were seeking help. I saw some people being mistreated, especially by two particular people of color. I had been told that African American people held negative views about Latinos and what I was looking at seemed to confirm what I had heard.

When it was my turn I was assigned a social worker. I didn't know which one would attend me, so I called on the Lord saying, *"Lord, please don't let an African American person serve me. I don't want to be rejected because I am Latino."*

As the minutes passed I intensified my prayer and in my heart I felt great anguish. At this point I had two enormous weights on my shoulders. The greatest one was the health and lives of my daughters. The other was the weight of the debt for their medical treatment that I had no idea how I would ever repay.

They finally called my name and there before me was an African American social worker. God had not heard my prayer, I thought. While I told my story one more time, the Holy Spirit came to my aid and clearly said to me, ***"Mention that you are a Christian, that you are a pastor and that you work with your church".*** She asked me several questions. *"Where do* *you work? With whom do you live? Where do you get your income?"* To each question I would add, *"Since I am a Christian, I live in the home of one of the brothers from the church." "Since I am a pastor, my church sends me my salary from my country... although they are behind six months"* etc. etc. The insistence of the Holy Spirit was so strong that I must have seemed like a broken record inserting "***Christian, pastor, church"*** into each of my answers.

After so many repetitive answers, the social worker said with a smile, *"Pastor, I am also a Christian and I go to church."*

"Oh!" I exclaimed. Now I understood why God was insisting that I underscore that I was a Christian. After asking me a few more questions, she left me to await a decision as to whether they could help me.

The half hour that I waited for the social worker to return was a very difficult experience for me. Finally she returned smiling. I wasn't sure how to interpret that smile until she said, *"Pastor, we are going to place your account in a special program called X02"*

To this day I have no idea what that means, but that program would cover the hospital costs of my daughters care retroactively and pay the rest of the hospital bills.

Glory to God! I was again witnessing a financial miracle. I looked at her and I just started crying. She came out from behind her desk and hugged me. Then she said, *"Let's pray! I'm going to ask one of the receptionists to join us because she is also a Christian!"* Quickly the receptionist enters and, lo and behold, it was the one I had seen before. The social worker told her my story and she let loose a portentous, ***"Halleluiah!"***

The three of us hugged and they cried with me. We gave thanks to the Lord for His mercy while our tears mixed together and our cheeks rubbed against each other in a joyous embrace. In Christ there is no Latino, or black or white person. His love makes us one.

That social worker became another one of my angels, even today the tears run down my cheeks as I recall that woman of God that was placed in our path as an instrument of this enormous miracle.

Within two weeks the cards that I would use to cover the hospital costs arrived. I went into Donna's office, the administrator of the clinic that treated those with AT (Ataxia Telangiectasia). She had told me on many occasions not to worry. She would joke with me to lift up my spirit saying, "*When all this is over, just go the airport and go home. Nobody is going all the way to Bolivia to bill you.*"

When she saw the insurance cards she took me by the hand and we went out headed for the finance office. We went down 11 floors of the pediatric building, passed through the main lobby and arrived at the accounting department. With great contentment, she had me by the hand the whole way. I have no idea what people might have thought seeing us walking linked together like that, the administrator of the world famous Johns Hopkins Hospital of Baltimore, Maryland, Donna emotionally passed all those corridors of the hospital holding hands with the father of those little female patients to show off the miracle to the accountants who needed to see payment for the hospital services. These very human moments, these noble moments that we experienced in the midst of our pain, made us feel like God and His angels were with us in the midst of the fiery furnace.

On arriving at the office, she searched for the person who was handling my account. This person responded by saying, *"I was just preparing a letter for Mr. Penaloza telling him that we were sending his account to a collection agency"*.

The bill was about 50 pages long filled with a long list of the charges that totaled **$230,000.**

With absolute confidence, Donna fanned out the insurance cards and said, *"Don't bother. Charge everything to these cards"*. The man looked at the cards, then he looked at me in total surprise and he said, *"How did you get these?"* All I could do was smile. It was my Lord who was preparing a table before my enemies. It was my Good Shepherd making sure that I wanted for nothing. It was His shadow that was guiding me through the valley of the shadow of death. For those who may not be familiar with Bible, this was Psalm 23 becoming a reality in my life.

It was Him!

MORE BLESSINGS FOR DANIELA

Daniela was receiving one treatment that caused her immunoglobulin counts to be normal for a whole month at a time. This treatment allowed Daniela to live the two best years of her life, healthy, alert, focused and full of life. Miriam had done an excellent job of planting our faith in her.

The church was again prospering. Members were being added and there arose a need to baptize the new members. On one of those baptism services that we did in October when it is no longer possible to ignore the cold weather, Daniela told her mother that she wanted to be baptized. Miriam unsuccessfully tried to make her understand that it was not possible because she could get sick and that we didn't want that to happen. Daniela insisted so much that she was at the point of tears. Miriam sent for me and told me of our daughter's desire to be baptized.

In order to discourage her, I placed her tiny feet in the water so she could feel how cold it was, but she had made her decision. She wanted to be baptized. We had to concede. She went under the water with confidence and peace. We lived a very reverent moment with her. Her baptism was her supernatural moment, her covenant moment with her God, the seal and confirmation of her citizenship of the New Jerusalem.

Daniela at her baptism

Daniela was present at the funeral of her two older siblings, Jose and Sara. When Miriam would tell the children that all of us would one day be in the presence of the Lord, Daniela was the one that always said that she wanted Jesus to come and take her. On various occasions she would ask her mother, *"Mommy, are you going to die?"* and Miriam would say yes. She would continue, *"Mommy, I'm going to die too?"* and Miriam would say yes. Daniela would say, *"Mommy, I want to die first"*. Miriam would say, *"It is very possible that that is what will happen, sweetheart"*. Daniela would continue, *"Mommy, I want to die before you, because I want you to sing at my funeral and I want lots of flowers and I don't want you to cry"*. Miriam would respond, *"That's fine, that's how we will do it..."*

DANIELA WAS PLANNING HER FUNERAL.

Daniela was very particular regarding her food and her entertainment. When she craved something to eat, she would eat that food everyday and for several weeks. When she wanted to see one of her animated videos, she would watch it for weeks, two or three times a day. So we knew videos like "Toy Story", "Beauty and the Beast" and others by heart. But above all she loved Barney, the Dinosaur. He was her favorite. She sang his songs and didn't miss his show every day. Her dream was to meet Barney. Miriam had taught my children that when papi couldn't buy them the things they wanted, they could pray and God would provide them with what they wanted ("*Ask and it shall be given to you...*") I am sure that at some point Daniela had asked God for the opportunity to meet Barney.

In the middle of the treatments, a nurse asked me if I had applied to the Make a Wish Foundation. I told her that I had never heard of it. She helped me with the paperwork and a few weeks later, a limousine picked us up at the house to take us to the airport where we boarded a plane to Orlando, to DISNEY WORLD! We had a week of free tickets to the shows, hotel and a personal visit with Barney.

Little Daniela was 7 years old and was in her wheelchair. They gave us special seating in the studios where the show was aired. Then after singing several songs, among them, "*I love you, you love me...*" which Daniela knew by heart (and so did we), we were asked to stay for a personal appointment with Barney. We were alone in the theatre. Daniela was relaxed. She didn't know what was coming. Suddenly the doors opened and there was the purple dinosaur. He came towards us and stood next to Daniela. He caressed her and played with her a little. Daniela looked like she was on cloud nine. Her joyous expression reminded me of that lost look common to young girls when they are in front of their idols. Our little daughter could not believe it! There was Barney just for her!

We enjoyed one of the loveliest moments in the life of our little girl and then Barney was gone. She had her dream come true. Once again God had surprised us with an unexpected gift.

CHAPTER 22

TIME TO DEPART

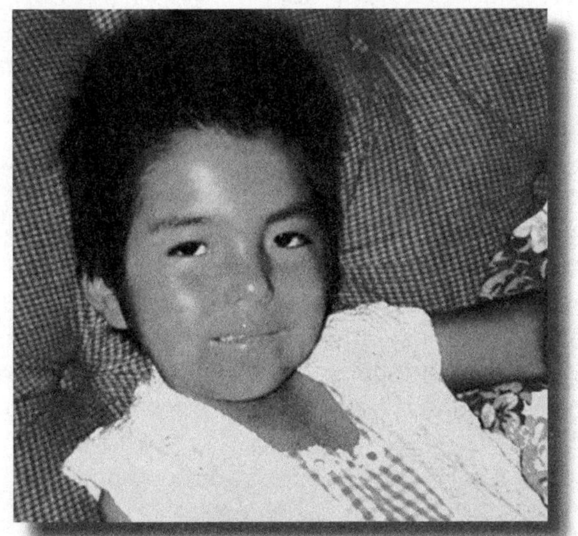

Daniela at 7 years old, a few weeks before her death

About a month after the wonderful experience with Barney, Daniela awoke one day very restless. She felt tired. She was hungry but she didn't want to do anything. It seemed strange to me. She had no fever. She was not sick. She had conquered her tumors once again with the use of an experimental drug. Everything seemed fine, but she did not feel fine. We took her to her pediatrician who was the wife of the oncologist who had done everything he could to keep Daniela alive. Dr. Lobe is another one of those angels that the Lord gave to bless us.

On the way to the hospital we got hungry. We stopped at a place in Maryland where they served this delicious chicken. Daniela didn't want any more, saying, "*No thank you. When we get home I will eat some more.*" She assumed that we would return the same day. Miriam and I looked at the other but said nothing. We asked ourselves, "*Will we return today?*"

Daniela's health got more complicated. Her lungs no longer functioned and she had to be intubated like little Sara had been. Within two or three weeks we were faced with the same situation as what we had experienced with Sara. Her lungs, her liver and her kidneys were failing. The doctors could do no more. Daniela was leaving us. The doctor could not understand. There was no infection, no tumors, and no cancer. There was nothing threatening her life, but Daniela was dying. Doctor Lobe said it was as if her little body was saying that it could go no further, that the hour of her departure was at hand.

From one moment to the next her room in intensive care in the pediatric building of the hospital was filled with doctors, nurses, specialists and scientists who in one way or the other had been involved with our case. All of them expressed their sympathy to us. The doctors instructed me on what was to happen. The nurses prepared Daniela. Miriam was at Daniela's bedside. Daniela was sedated. She was already more dead than alive.

I wanted to ask Dr. Lobe something, but I couldn't find him. I saw Miriam who at this point had left Daniela's side when suddenly this thought burst into my head, "*Daniela is my last daughter*".

She and Sara had been so close to each other, I instinctively went to the head of Daniela's bed. I spoke to Daniela in the same way that Miriam had done with Sara two years earlier. *"Daniela,"* I said, *"Today you will be with our Lord in heaven. Today you will see your brother and sisters and today your walk on this earth will end. You know how much we love you, but your mom especially loves you.*

The minute you see Jesus, speak to Him and ask Him to help your mommy to handle your loss, because I think it will be very difficult for her".

I left her side one more time and when I returned, I saw her oncologist, Dr. Lobe. He saw me and we could not hold back the tears. He had poured all of his professional experience and strength into our case. We could feel it. We had developed a great affection for him.

The infilling of the Holy Spirit gave us the strength necessary to go through this moment of Daniela's passing into eternity. They disconnected her, placed her in our laps and we waited for her heart to stop beating. Once again, loving words came from Miriam's lips as she said good-bye to her last child. We placed her in her bed knowing that she was being taken by her heavenly angels into the presence of her Creator.

Miriam and I went down to the cafeteria, where we had so often bought individual pizzas for Daniela when it was the only food she could eat for days on end. We bought coffee and sitting there; suddenly Miriam looked at me and said, *"I feel such a great joy, a profound happiness. I know my daughter has already arrived in heaven and that she is fine".* It was heavenly wine, the Holy Spirit who, in answer to our petition, had poured over Miriam's heart, converting our sadness into joy, our grief into happiness, and our loss into victory.

Every parent knows that each child is unique and has his or her own characteristics. With Daniela this was particularly true. She was obedient and quick. She made the most of every moment. She was quicker than all her siblings and now was no exception. She had made it to heaven, seen Jesus and promptly carried out the task that her father gave her, asking God to help her mother. Not even half an hour after her death, the answer was already evident. We were sitting in the cafeteria of the hospital. We had just lost all the heirs that we had on this earth. We no longer had children here. In the natural there was no reason why we should be happy, but Miriam and I are part of a supernatural world. Although we were born in this world, we do not belong to it. This is what happens with all of those who have been born again by the love and mercy of God.

For us death was not the end. For us it was an ugly and disfigured attendant who only opens the door to eternity so that those of us, who are washed by the precious blood of Jesus, can come into the fullness of joy with our Lord.

By this time Ekklesia USA had a large membership and also had the human resources and funds available to help its pastor. Our leaders took charge of all the arrangements for the funeral. Thank God for the marvelous brothers and sisters who made a covenant with the Lord and with the house of God where we presided as pastors. We are so very grateful for their unconditional love, their service and dedication. More than this we feel that we owe a debt even greater than gratitude...a debt of love.

Daniela's funeral was very special. We celebrated it in the church in Vienna, Virginia. There was peace and rejoicing. The arrangements were already made. The voices of the praise team filled the atmosphere with worship. There were lots of flowers exactly as Daniela had requested.

Miriam was standing by my side. I cried freely. The presence of God was intense. Suddenly Miriam asked me if she could sing with the praise team because she could not contain the joy that overcame her. I told her that it was ok and her face was shining with the glory of God. She looked like an angel. She did not shed one tear exactly as her daughter had requested.

Carlos, Miriam and Betty Strombeck at Daniela's funeral

Daniela had not asked me for anything so I was free to cry. Once again the Lord responded to us even in the smallest details that His little daughter, Daniela, had requested.

In a moment of spiritual understanding, I became aware of the fact that death was absent at the funeral. There was joy, victory, consolation and love from God. Life was present!

The Bible speaks of the blessings in the New Testament. It says that blessed are the poor in Spirit for theirs is the kingdom of heaven.

I think that they are poor because they have given everything and have kept nothing. However, having nothing, they have remained faithful to their Lord and God by His love; though He owes nothing to anyone He gives them the kingdom of heaven. That's how Miriam and I felt. We were made poor by having given everything for the Kingdom, but we are heirs of that same kingdom because we had remained faithful. As the apostle Paul said, *"For to me to live is Christ and to die is gain." Philippians 1: 21*

We remain poor because we owe so much to so many flesh and blood angels that a lifetime of gratitude would never come close to repaying, but we can give what we have and what we have is the Kingdom of God, the consolation of the Spirit and THE VICTORY OVER DEATH.

Epilogue

Carlos, ministering in the church

Several years have passed since the passing of all our children into the presence of God. Miriam and I have shared our testimony many times and each time we have been witnesses to the marvelous work of God in the lives of our audiences. Some receive consolation for the loss of a loved one which they could not previously understand. Others receive clarification on the subject of suffering. Still others come to understand the why behind incomprehensible situations and they end up admiring God for His powerful support in the middle of a crisis. Sometimes only silent tears simply express gratitude for the grace of God that is present for us in every moment while understanding that it is also real for our personal situations.

Someone once described me as the *"New Testament Job"*. I have identified myself with many of the experiences of Job. Especially with the part where his children died and how at the end of the story, God restores Job and awards him a double portion of what he previously had. How many of us long for a double portion of what He gives us? However, to obtain it many times we must first lose everything.

Carlos as he is today

Meditating on this book of the Bible, we see that when the time comes to restore what was lost, God gave Job ten children. A question arose in me, or perhaps, better said, an argument:

to his children did you only give him ten? Shouldn't it have been twenty because Job lost ten children in the beginning?

The many lessons we learned during this pilgrimage are precious and I would like to add a few more that I think will be of interest to the reader. One more time His response left me speechless. God said to me,

"The ten children that died were not lost. They slept and are in my presence. Adding those to the ones I gave him in the end, makes a total of twenty. So what is your question?"

Then I understood and it was confirmed one more time that the children who die in Christ, really are just sleeping! They are in the presence of God! We shall see them once again! We shall hold them in our arms again!

This conviction is a consolation. They are not dead. They sleep and shall rise again. Like the lyrics in the old hymn says,

"When the trumpet of the Lord shall sound, and time shall be no more, And the morning breaks, eternal, bright and fair; When the saved of earth shall gather over on the other shore, And the roll is called up yonder, I'll be there." Death is swallowed up in victory. Halleluia!

If you have young children, are you preparing them for eternity? It is never too early to begin. No matter how short the lives of men are, God created a purpose for each one. The foot-print they leave behind when they die motivates and inspires us to face life.

Miriam as she is today

"And we know that for those who love God all things work together for good, for those who are called according to his purpose." Romans 8:28

That purpose has to do with the message that God is developing through your life. The more difficult the experiences, however more difficult your life, the deeper the sacrifice.

God is even more sufficient. The message that He speaks through your life becomes stronger and more powerful.

Many have said to us that if they had to go through what we went through, they could not have gone on. In a way this is true, because the challenges of one do not have to be faced by others and that is why God does not give us more than we can handle. We have the assurance that surely through the challenge He will provide a way out.

Miriam and I didn't know that we had the strength to withstand this process. We never imagined that we would face a challenge like this in our lives, but while we were in the fiery furnace, His grace was sufficient for us. It is like when He told Paul, "*My grace is sufficient for you...*"

Miriam ministering in the church

Statistics show that 95% of marriages involving the death of a child end in divorce. This is probably because each spouse holds the other responsible for the loss or because the void left by the child can't be filled with anything else. That emptiness ends up destroying the marriage. In our case, after 29 years of marriage in which Miriam and I have served the Lord, the words of our marriage vows have been tested to the maximum. *"For better or for worse, in sickness and in health, for richer or poorer until death do us part…"* No. The difficulty of our experiences could not separate us. Death did not separate us because when it wanted to overwhelm us, thanks to the supernatural intervention of God, the confession of Paul the Apostle became reality to us.

"No, in all these things we are more than conquerors through him who loved us. For I am sure that neither death nor life, nor angels nor rulers, nor things present nor things to come, nor powers, nor height nor depth, nor anything else in all creation, will be able to separate us from the love of God in Christ Jesus our Lord."

Romans 8:37-39

Carlos and Miriam – 2012

Sometimes when I think about the possibility that I could have avoided all that awaited me when I told the Lord that I would serve Him, and if He had asked me if I still wanted to continue, I probably would have said no. However, on this side of the victory, I don't regret serving Him and walking with Him with what He had planned from the beginning. Everything that we have lived through has allowed us to encounter an invisible God as our sustenance. We learned to recognize Him as the **ALL SUFFICIENT GOD** in all the experiences of our lives, a God who brings victory out of what appears to be defeat..., a God who keeps us firmly committed and who without regard to our experiences, keeps His promise: I am with you until the end of the earth, and that "I am with you" is not passive like an observer, but He is completely and profoundly "involved" in every moment of our lives. He allowed us to know Him in a way that we would not have known Him if circumstances had not been as they were.

It was this conviction that allowed us to experience the other face of victory. The love of God which is real in our lives, the love that gives us the strength to conquer what appears to be invincible, to go on where others stop, to feel joy while others are bitter in their pain. That love changes us into the heroes of the faith like those heroes in Hebrews 11, like the first century Christians who for that love faced lions and fire.

Because of this, beloved reader, I cannot finish this testimony without inviting you to make Jesus your companion in life no matter what the situation in your life may be. He will convert it into a glorious adventure that will allow you to experience His companionship, His support, His love, His wisdom and His grace.

I am sure that your life will enter into a supernatural dimension where the culmination of the words in 2 Corinthians 5:17 will come true.

"Therefore, if anyone is in Christ, he is a new creation. The old has passed away; behold, the new has come...."

If this is your sincere desire, join me in this prayer:

"Lord Jesus forgive me if at some point I have thought that you have abandoned me or if I believed that you had forgotten me and that you didn't care about my suffering or the circumstances that I faced, when in reality You were at my side every step of the way even if I didn't see You. Now I understand your great love for me. Thank you for your forgiveness. Today I

give myself to You and I ask you to write my name in the book of life. I consecrate myself to you and I beg you to be with me in all the circumstances of my life and to permit me to know you in all I experience, knowing that You make all things work for good. Amen.

Welcome to a real life where despite all, the other face of victory is marvelous!

Carlos Peñaloza